William Willis

Genealogy of the Mckinstry Family

With a Preliminary Essay on the Scotch-Irish Immigrations to America

William Willis

Genealogy of the Mckinstry Family
With a Preliminary Essay on the Scotch-Irish Immigrations to America

ISBN/EAN: 9783337404314

Printed in Europe, USA, Canada, Australia, Japan

Cover: Foto ©Suzi / pixelio.de

More available books at **www.hansebooks.com**

GENEALOGY

OF THE

McKINSTRY FAMILY,

WITH

A PRELIMINARY ESSAY

Scotch-Irish Immigrations to America.

BY WILLIAM WILLIS,

OF PORTLAND, ME.

———

SECOND EDITION:
CORRECTED AND ENLARGED.

———

THE McKINSTRY FAMILY.

The McKINSTRYS originated in Scotland. The first of the name who emigrated to Ireland was Rodger, who had lived in the neighborhood of Edinburgh, and emigrated thence to the north of Ireland about the year 1669. I propose, as a preliminary to the history of this family, to give a brief account of the Scotch emigration to Ireland, and from that country to America previous to our Revolution.

During the Irish rebellions in the reign of Elizabeth, the Province of Ulster, embracing the northern counties of Ireland, was greatly depopulated, and it became a favorite project with her successor, James I., to repeople those counties with a protestant population, the better to preserve order, and introduce a higher state of cultivation in that portion of his dominions. To promote this object, liberal offers of land were made, and other inducements held out in England and Scotland, for persons to occupy this wide and vacant territory. The project was eagerly embraced; companies and colonies were formed, and individuals without organization were tempted to partake of the advantageous offers of government. A London company, among the first to enter upon this new acquisition, established itself at Derry, and gave such a character to the place as to cause it to be afterwards and forever known as the renowned city of Londonderry.

The first emigration from Scotland was chiefly from the Highlands, where agricultural resources were scanty and often wholly cut off, and where the fruits of labor were gathered from a stern soil. Sir Hugh Montgomery, the sixth Laird of Braidstone, a friend and follower of King James, was among the earliest to obtain possession of forfeited land in the county of Down, and laid his rough hand upon many broad acres. The coast of Scotland is within twenty miles of the county of Antrim in Ireland, and across this frith or strait flowed from the northeast a population distinguished for thrift, industry and endurance, which has given a peculiar and elevated character to that portion of the emerald island. It is said that the clan McDonald contributed largely to this emigration, and was among the first of the Scottish nation to plant upon its shores. They scattered chiefly in the counties of Down, Londonderry and Antrim, and greatly assisted to build up Newry, Bangor, Derry and Belfast, the principal cities of those counties.

This was the first protestant population that was introduced into Ireland, the Presbyterians of Scotland furnishing the largest element; and they have maintained their ascendancy to the present day, against the persevering efforts of the Episcopalians on the one hand, and of the Romanists, bigoted and numerous, by whom they were surrounded, on the other. The first Presbyterian church established in Ireland was in Ballycarry, in the county of Antrim, in 1613.

The clan Alpine, otherwise called the McGregors, in the latter part of the 17th century, had made themselves very obnoxious to government and the neighboring clans by a wild and reckless course of life. Argyle, the chief of the Campbells, their inveterate enemy, who was high in court favor, procured a decree of extermination against them, extending even to the obliteration of their name and place of residence. Heavy penalties were proclaimed against all who bore the badge of the clan. To avoid this withering persecution, many sought refuge in the neighboring islands; many changed their names and fled to remote parts of their own country or to other countries. Descedants from this clan are now found in the United States and elsewhere, under the names of Grier, Greer, Gregor, Gregory, &c., the Mac being dropped. Thus we shall probably find that a distinguished Judge of the Supreme Court of the U. States, residing in Pennsylvania, Judge Grier, derives his origin from the same wild tribe, which, under the guidance of Robroy McGregor, was the terror of the high and low lands of his native soil. Nor was the change of name confined to that clan; for we are assured that the Mackinnons, from the isle of Skye, are now McKenna, McKean, McCannon; that McNish has become McNiece, Meness, Munniss, and Moniss; and Graham is Graeme, Grimes, Groom, &c.

Although the rebellions of 1715 and 1745, against the House of Hanover, made large additions to the Scotch population in the north of Ireland, yet by far the largest accessions to this colonization were occasioned by religious persecutions in the time of the latter Stuarts. That fated race, blind to the dictates of justice and humanity, and devoted with sullen bigotry to their peculiar notions in religion and politics, pursued a system of measures best calculated to wean from their support subjects the most devoted to their cause. The Scottish race was bound to the Stuarts by a national prejudice and a sincere affection. But they were imbued with a religious enthusiasm, inspired by Knox their great apostle, which ruled their consciences, and rendered the sanctions of a higher law superior to their patriotism, or their attachment to their native sovereigns. Rather, they believed that true patriotism consisted in maintaining the religion transmitted by their fathers.

When, therefore, the Charleses and James II. endeavored to introduce prelacy among them, and to force it upon their consciences by arbitrary laws and the iron hoofs of the dragoons of Claverhouse, very many of these hardy, persistent and enduring Presbyterians, having suffered to the bitter end of cruelty and oppression, abandoned the land of their birth, the home of their fondest affections, and sought an asylum among their countrymen in the secure retreats of Ulster, or fled across the ocean. They carried their household gods with them; and their religious peculiarities became more dear in their land of exile, for the dangers and sorrows through which they had borne them.

Presbyterianism was transported from Geneva to Scotland by John Knox, who composed the first Book of Discipline, containing the substance of his intended policy, in 1561. In 1566, a general assembly approved the Discipline; and all church affairs, after that time, were managed by Presbyteries and General Assemblies. They did not at first formally deprive the bishops, who had ecclesiastical jurisdiction, of their power, but they went on gradually and steadily doing it, as they acquired confidence and strength. In 1574, they voted bishops to be only pastors of one parish; in 1577, they decreed that bishops should be called by their own names without title; and the next year they declared the name of bishop to be a nuisance. In 1580, they pronounced with one voice, in the General Assembly, that diocesan episcopacy was unscriptural and unlawful. The same year, King James and his family, with the whole Scotch nation, subscribed a confession of faith, embracing the "solemn league and covenant," obliging them to maintain the protestant doctrine and presbyterian government. Thus, in the space of twenty years, grew up this formal, extensive and powerful institution, twining itself over the Scottish mind with stern and inflexible bands, which death only could sunder; and for which, home, country, life—all things beside—were freely given up.

James had hardly become secure and easy on his English throne when he began his attack upon the religious system of his early life, and of his native country, and his successors followed it up with a pertinacity worthy of a better cause. The attempts to establish the church of England over Scotland, and destroy the religious system so universally established and so dearly cherished by that devoted people, was pursued by the Charleses and James the 2d, by persecutions as mean, as cruel, and savage, as any which have disgraced the annals of religious bigotry and crime. And they did not cease until they had greatly depopulated Scotland, and were stripped of their power by the happy revolution under William and Mary, which restored repose to a distracted and long suffering people.

Scotland, a country no larger than Maine, with a population at the close of the seventeenth century of a million, and in 1800 not so much as the present population of Massachusetts and Maine;* with agricultural and

---

* The area of Scotland is 31,324 square miles, that of Maine is 31,766. The population of Scotland in 1851 was 2,889,742; of Massachusetts and Maine in 1860, 1,859,501.

other resources by no means equal to ours—of which a writer in a recent number of the Edinburgh Review, on the Highlands, says, "at the end of the 17th century the chief social feature of the Highlands was famine, and another was emigration." Yet this country has contributed largely, by emigration, to furnish numerous and prominent settlers for many other lands; to the nation with which she is connected, profound statesmen, brilliant writers, and men the most renowned in every department of scientific and philosophical research.

This is the race, composed of various tribes flowing from different parts of Scotland, which furnished the materials of the Scotch-Irish immigration to this country. By their industry, frugality and skill, they had made the deserted region into which they had moved, a comparatively rich and flourishing country. They had improved agriculture and introduced manufactures, and by the excellence and high reputation of their productions had attracted trade and commerce to their markets, so as to excite the jealousy of government in the reigns of Anne and the first George, notwithstanding that by their efforts and example the prosperity of the whole island had been promoted. The patronizing government began to recognize them, in the shape of taxes and embarrassing regulations upon their industry and trade. The same jealousy controlled that government afterwards, in regard to the American Colonies, by which the commerce and enterprise of their subjects on this side of the ocean, were, in like manner, hampered and restricted, so that they were hardly permitted to manufacture articles of the most common necessity, but were driven to import them from the mother country, as glass, nails, hats, cloths, &c.

These restrictions occasioned general distress, not only in the north of Ireland, but throughout the whole island. To this, Douglass (p. 368) says, "was added an extravagant advance in rents by landlords, whose long leases were now expired." The energetic and self-willed population of the north of Ireland, animated by the same spirit which subsequently moved the American mind, determined no longer to endure these oppressive measures; and they sought by another change to find a freer verge for the exercise of their industry and skill, and for the enjoyment of their religion.

One of their spiritual leaders, the Rev. David McGregor, in a sermon which he preached on the eve of the departure from Ireland, assigned the following reasons for their removal to America: 1, to avoid oppressive and cruel bondage; 2, to shun persecution; 3, to withdraw from the communion of idolaters; 4, to have an opportunity of worshipping God according to the dictates of conscience and his inspired word. He looked at it chiefly from a religious point of view; others, from a material and commercial standpoint. It was undoubtedly suggested and promoted by a variety of motives gradually operating upon the mass of the population, which brought them to the determination, solemn and painful, to sunder the ties which had bound them firmly to their adopted country, and impelled them to seek new and doubtful homes in a wild, unexplored, and far-distant land.

The first immigration of these people to this country was to the Middle and Southern Colonies. As early as 1684 a settlement was formed in New Jersey, and in 1690 small groups were found in the Carolinas, Maryland and Pennsylvania. It seems to be well established that the first Presbyterian church in the United States was formed by a company of Scotch immigrants in Upper Marlborough, Maryland, about the year 1690. Another about the same time at Snowhill in the same State. In 1692, two churches of this denomination were established in Freehold and Woodbridge, in New Jersey, one composed of Scotch, the other of Scotch and New England immigrants. But it was not until the reigns of Anne and George I. that large numbers, driven by oppressive measures of government and disastrous seasons, were induced to seek, even in the wilderness, a better home than their old settled region could give them. Gordon says, " Scarcity of corn, generally prevalent from the discouragement of industry, amounted in 1728 and the following year almost to a famine, especially in Ulster. Emigrations to America, which have since increased, drew above 3000 people annually from Ulster alone." Dr. Boulter, afterwards Archbishop of Armagh, who labored strenuously in 1728 to divert the horrors of famine in Ireland, wrote to the English ministry, March 7, 1728, that there were seven ships then lying at Belfast that " are carrying off about 1000 passengers ; most of them can neither get victuals nor work at home." He also says, " 3100 men, women and children went from Ireland to America in 1727, and 4200 in three years, all protestants." The principal seats of these emigrations were Pennsylvania and the Middle States. New England was found not so favorable to their farming and other interests. Douglass, who wrote at Boston in 1750, says, " at first they chose New England, but being brought up to husbandry, &c., New England did not answer so well as the Colonies southward ; at present they generally resort to Pennsylvania." By Proud's history of Pennsylvania, we find that in 1729 near 6000 arrived in that Colony ; and before the middle of the century nearly 12.000 arrived annually for several years. These were protestants and generally Presbyterians ; few or no Catholics came, until some time after the Revolution.

In the summer of 1718, the first organized company of this class of immigrants, of which we have any knowledge, left the shores of Ireland in five vessels, containing 120 families, for the new world, and arrived safely in Boston, August 4, 1718. Here all was new, the wilderness and the world before them. Imagine this little colony, strangers in a strange land, seeking new homes and not knowing whither to turn. There they, lie at the little wharf at the foot of State street in the town of Boston, which then contained about 12,000 inhabitants, taking counsel where to go, and how to dispose of themselves and their little ones, to begin the world anew. With their wonted energy, they were soon astir. One brigantine, with a company of twenty families, sought their fortunes at the eastward, among whom were Armstrong, Means, McKean, Gregg ;— they spent a hard and long winter in Portland harbor, and then fled westward, most of them, to join their companions in founding their new Londonderry. Another portion went to Andover and its neighborhood, led on by their pastor, McGregor ; another to Pelham, Mass., under the lead of the Rev. Ralph Abercrombie ; another remained in Boston, under their pastor, the Rev. John Moorhead ; and still another sought refuge in Worcester and vicinity. Wherever they went, this devoted people first of all planted the Presbyterian church, adopting the discipline and usages of the church of Scotland. Mr. McGregor and his flock finally established themselves at Nutfield, N. H., and built up a town which they called, from their venerated city in Ireland, Londonderry. Here they founded a colony, which, like a fruitful mother, has been sending forth from its prolific bosom men and women, of their hardy and enlightened stock, to instruct and adorn society. And here were gathered the McGregors, McClintocks, Starks, Reid, Bell, Morrison, Anderson, McKean, and others, who have given vigor to our varied institutions.

The society in Boston established the Presbyterian church, which continued for more than half a century to worship in their meeting-house on the corner of Long Lane, now Federal street, and Bury street, where Dr. Gannett's church stood until 1859, under the pastoral care of Rev. John Moorhead, familiarly called Johnny Moorhead, whose ardent and impulsive temper often led him into embarrassments, but who faithfully ministered to his people until his death in 1773. He was succeeded by the Rev. Robert Annan, a Scotch presbyter, who occupied the pulpit until 1786, when the people cast off Presbyterianism, assumed the Congregational form of government, and, in 1787, settled the excellent and learned Dr. Jeremy Belknap. In April, 1745, Messrs. Moorhead, McGregor, Abercrombie, with James McKean and others, met at Londonderry and established the first Presbytery in New England, consisting of twelve churches, called the Presbytery of Boston.

This company introduced into Boston the cultivation of the potato, which had not before been known in the country, and the flax spinning wheel, the familiar domestic instrument of their native households. The latter had quite a run in Boston ; schools were established to teach the art of spinning, and ladies of the first quality were found among the votaries of this useful art.

The party which went to Worcester fared worse than any other ; they encountered a severe persecution, and were not permitted to erect a house of worship of their peculiar order. In one attempt of the kind, the structure was entirely demolished by a mob. A great prejudice was enlisted against them, both from their religion and their country; they were called *Irish*, a term they greatly resented. Mr. McGregor wrote, "We are surprised to hear ourselves termed Irish people." The Worcester immigrants struggled awhile against a bitter opposition, and finding repose there hopeless, they abandoned the place, some for Pelham, others for their head-quarters in Londonderry, and some to plant themselves at Unadilla, on the banks of the Susquehanna, in New York. In the Worcester company were the names of Clark, McKinstry, Gray, Ferguson, Crawford, Graham, Barbour, Blair, and Thornton; Mathew Thornton, then a child, became the distinguished patriot and statesman of New Hampshire, and a signer of the declaration of Independence.

In 1719 and 1720, five ships, under the conduct of Capt. Robert Temple, who had previously explored the country, landed several hundred families from Ireland on the shores of Kennebec river and Merry Meeting Bay. Temple was of a distinguished family in Ireland, and the ancestor of the numerous and respectable family of the late Lt. Governor Thomas L. Winthrop, of Boston, who married his grand-daughter Elizabeth Bowdoin.

Dummer's Indian war broke up this colony, and the larger part of them went to Pennsylvania. After the war was ended, other companies of this race occupied various points in Maine, as Topsham, Brunswick, Boothbay, Pemaquid, and the Waldo patent, which region contained a larger number of this description of immigrants than any part of New England. In 1771, a Presbytery was established at Boothbay called the Presbytery of the Eastward, consisting of three ministers and four Ruling Elders, representing four churches. It never consisted of more than eight ministers, and the last record of it now known to exist, was an adjournment to meet at New Boston, in New Hampshire, on the first Wednesday in October, 1792. They were entirely under the religious government of Presbyters and Assemblies, until the eve of the Revolution, when large accessions of Congregationalists or Independents mingling among them, a struggle took place between the two orders for the government of the church. This resulted in the overthrow of Presbyterianism and the establishment of Congregationalism over the churches of the State. There is not now a Presbyterian church in Maine. Once it boasted of Murray, famed for his eloquence,—of Rutherford, Blair, Boyd, Dunlap, McLean, Urquahart, Whittaker, Strickland,—none remain, and hardly a record of them. The same struggle took place in Massachusetts, until Synod, Presbytery and Church disappeared, and now only the feeble Presbytery of Londonderry remains in New England to record and perpetuate the religious characteristics of that great race which sought refuge on these shores, and has done so much to advance the honor and prosperity of the country. Their power as a sect is most prevalent in the Middle and Western States.

In 1805 the Presbytery of Londonderry consisted of eleven churches, of which three were in Massachusetts, and twenty-eight ministers, but only nine of the ministers had a pastoral charge. Seven of these were pastors of Congregational churches, and six were supposed to be Congregational ministers, of whom one was in Massachusetts, three in N. H. and two in Maine.

Independency or Congregationalism was not introduced into England until 1616. But Puritanism, which embraces both orders of dissenters, had its origin in Elizabeth's time, in her attempts to cause subscriptions to be made to the liturgy, ceremonies, and discipline of the Church, in 1564. Those who refused subscription and preferred a simple worship, were called Puritans by way of reproach. When the doctrines of Arminius began to prevail in the English church, the Puritans adhered to the system of Calvin, and were defined to be men of severe morals, Calvinists in doctrine, and non-conformists to the ceremonies and discipline of the Church. The first Presbyterian church was established in England, near London, in 1577, by a few scattered brethren ; and both these branches of dissenters, Independents and Presbyterians, made at first but slow progress ; and although agreeing in doctrine, they differed from each other on the form of government as widely as they both did from Episcopacy.

The Independents or Congregational brethren were small in number in the Westminster Assembly, although they increased prodigiously afterwards under Cromwell. They made a bold stand against the proceedings of the high Presbyterians. They maintained " that every particular congregation of Christians" has an entire and complete power of jurisdiction over its members, to be exercised by the elders thereof within itself." They add, "this they are sure must have been the form of government in the primitive church."—*Neal*, 3, 157.

The system of the Independents was attacked by the rigid Presbyterians with great severity, " as tending to break the uniformity of the church, under pretence of liberty of conscience." But one of their number, Mr. Herle, the prolocutor of the Assembly, with great candor and good sense, remarked, " The difference between us and our brethren who are for Independency, is nothing so great as some conceive ; at most, it does but ruffle the fringe, not any way rend the garment of Christ."

Yet the quarrel continued, and has continued to the present day ; the sound of the controversy, even in this country, is now ringing in our ears ; in the last century it was discordant and harsh throughout our churches in the ambitious struggle for power. The controversy then related to church government, for in doctrine there was a substantial agreement. The Savoy confession of 1658 proceeds upon the plan of the Westminster Assembly ; the preface declares, " that they fully consent to the Westminster confession, for the substance of it." The disagreement was not in matters of faith, but only in matters of form.

It is not my intention to trace further the migrations of these people upon this continent. Having accompanied the earliest colony to Massachusetts, which contained the first of the McKinstry family who came to America, I leave the nation to follow the fortunes of the individual.

I. JOHN McKINSTRY, the first of the name who came to this country, was born in Brode Parish, in the county of Antrim, Ireland, in 1677. He was of Scotch descent, and was the son of Rodger McKinstry and Mary Wilson, who lived in the neighborhood of Edinburgh, until compelled by the persecutions under Charles II., about 1669, to seek security and repose with their Presbyterian brethren in the province of Ulster, and the county of Antrim. The analysis of the name is *Mac*, of or son of *Kin*, head or chief man *stræ*, of the stræth or valley This indicates a common origin with the old Scottish name, MacKenzie. The MacKinstry name is not uncommon at the present time, in Ireland, and also in Scotland. We find in Armagh, a solicitor by the name of John, and in the county of Longford, there are several bearing the name of John, Alexander and Robert, familiar also in the families in this country. The grand-father of John of Armagh, migrated from Antrim.

John, the son of Roger above named, was educated at the University of Edinburgh, from which he graduated Master of Arts in 1712. It may gratify the curious to see the Diploma which that University then granted to its graduates, which we annex in the original language :—

" Ne quem forte habeat cujus scire interest, Nos Universitatis—Jacobi Regis Edinensis Professores Testamur hunc Juvenem Johannem Mc-Kinstrie Hibernum, Post quam Philosophiæ & Humanioribus Literis ea Morum Integritate et Modestia (quæ Ingenuum decebat Adolescentem) apud. Nos vacasset, eaque præstitisset, omnia quæ Disciplinæ Ratio et Academiæ consuetudo præscripserat ; Tandem consensu Senatus Academici Magistrum in Artibus Liberalibus Riti Renunciatum, Cunctaque consecutum Privelegia quæ Bonarum Artium Magistris uspiam concedi solent: Cujus Rei quo major esset fides, Sigillum Inclyti Senatores Edinensis Athenæi Curatores et Patroni Nos Chirographa Apposuimus IV. Kal Martii MDCCII. Datum Edinburgi.

JOH. GOODALL, L. S. P.
ROBERTUS HENDERSON B & Acad. ab Archivi.
GULIEL. HAMILTON, N. S. P.
GULIELMUS LAW, P. P.
GULIELMUS SCOTT, P. P.
ROBERTUS STOUAOL, P. P.
COL: DRUMOND, P. P.
JA: GREGORY, Math. P."

Translation.—" Be it known to all whom it may concern, that we, the Professors of the University of Edinboro' of King James, testify, that this youth, John McKinstry of Ireland, after having completed the study of philosophy and human literature with the integrity and modesty of manners which is becoming an ingenuous youth, has graduated with us, and is entitled to all the privileges which the course of discipline and the custom of this Academy is accustomed to confer. And now, with the consent of the Faculty and teachers of this College, he is declared a Master in the liberal Arts, and entitled to all the privileges which are wont to be conceded to the Masters of the Good Arts. Of which fact, that there may be greater faith, we, the distinguished Governors, Teachers and Patrons of the University of Edinburgh, have placed our signatures, this 4th Calends of March, 1712."

How he disposed of himself for the next six years we have no information; he certainly qualified himself for the ministry, and undoubtedly received Presbyterian ordination. He joined the company of emigrants from the north of Ireland in the summer of 1718, and arrived in Boston, August 4, 1718. He followed the fortunes of that portion of the immigrants which went to Worcester county. He had not long been there before his services were sought by the people of Sutton, a new town near Worcester, the settlement of which had just commenced. At a meeting of the inhabitants, Nov. 25, 1719, it was voted that Mr. McKinstry should preach three months, and have fifteen pounds for the service. In the following March, the town voted to settle Mr. McKinstry, and to pay him £60 a year salary. In pursuance of this and other votes, he was duly settled according to Congregational usage on the 9th of November, 1720, neighboring churches being present and assisting in the ordination; the Rev. Mr. Swift of Framingham gave the Charge and the Rev. Mr. Thatcher of Milton, the Right hand of Fellowship. The people were generally Congregationalists, while the pastor, born and educated in rigid Presbyterianism, could not, in his new position, lay aside his attachments to the religious usages of his life. Difficulties therefore arose soon after his settlement, on these opposite views of church government, which produced continued uneasiness in the parish; a Council was called in October, 1726, to which twelve respected members of the church entered their dissent on the ground that nothing was charged against him. There is no record of the action of the Council, but the dissatisfaction continued and led to a separation in September, 1728. During his ministry at Sutton of less than eight years, forty-four members were added to the church. The Rev. Mr. Tracy, in an historical sermon preached to the parishioners in 1842, says of Mr. McKinstry, that "he was a man of considerable brilliancy and popular talent." On leaving Sutton Mr. McKinstry concluded to join his brethren of the same denomination in New York. On his way thither, his wife's health failing, he rested at East Windsor in Connecticut. The parish in the eastern precinct of the town, afterwards called Ellington, having no preacher, he was requested to supply the pulpit. This circumstance resulted in a suspension of his journey southward, and a settlement over that parish, as its first pastor, in 1733. He continued in this situation sixteen years, and remained in the town until his death, which took place on Sunday, January 20, 1754, at the age of 77 years. He preached on the Sunday previous to his death. Mr. McKinstry is said to have been a gentleman of good abilities, of popular talents, and unwavering integrity, a quality belonging to the family. His wife died Oct. 25, 1782, aged 81. Wm. McKinstry, of Middletown, Con., the only surviving grand-child of the first John, in 1859, erected a handsome granite monument over the graves of his grand-parents, in the ancient cemetery of Ellington, with appropriate inscriptions.

Soon after his settlement in Sutton, he married Elizabeth Fairfield, of Wenham, Mass., probably a daughter of William Fairfield, who represented his town in the General Court twenty-seven years, in nine of which he was Speaker of the House. Mr. Fairfield's oldest son William, died in Boston in 1770, leaving six children, the second of whom, the Rev. Wm. Fairfield, born in Boston in 1736, was settled in the ministry at Saco, Maine, in 1762. He was grand-father of the late Gov. Fairfield, of Maine. Mr. McKinstry had by her, seven children, viz: *John*, born Dec. 31, 1723; *Mary*, b. Jan. 1, 1726; *Alexander*, b. May 16, 1729; *William*, b. Oct. 8, 1732; *Paul*, b. Sept. 18, 1734; *Elizabeth*, b. May 27, 1736; *Abigail*, b. March 5, 1739. The first two in Sutton, the others in Ellington.

Elizabeth and Abigail died unmarried, the latter in Ellington, May 18, 1814. Elizabeth was killed by Bristol, a negro servant of her brother William, June 4, 1763, while she was visiting him in Taunton. The negro was fond of Elizabeth, but had been made to believe that he could obtain his freedom by killing some one of the family. He therefore took an opportunity, when his victim's back was towards him, and struck her a fatal blow on the back of her head with a flat-iron. Much excitement was produced in that quiet village and throughout the county by this sad event; and a great crowd attended upon his trial and execution, which soon after followed.

The other five children were married and left issue, as we proceed to describe:—

II. JOHN, eldest son of Rev. John of Ellington, was born in Sutton December 31, 1723; he graduated at Yale College in 1746, a classmate and chum of Ezra Stiles, afterwards the distinguished President of the College. Students at that time were placed on the catalogue according to the rank of their parents; McKinstry was placed fourth in a class of twelve; he survived all his classmates by fifteen years, and died Nov. 9, 1813, at the age of 90. He was ordained the first pastor of the 5th church in Springfield, which is now Chicopee, Mass., Sept. 27, 1752; the parish was incorporated June 10, 1751. The church at the time of his ordination consisted of 43 members. His father, then seventy-five years old, attended the ordination, as did also the following clergymen, Messrs: Stephen Williams of Longmeadow, Samuel Hopkins of West Springfield, Peter Reynolds, of Enfield, Robert Brock of Springfield and Noah Merrick of Wilbraham. His salary was £80 settlement, and £45 a year for the first ten years, with 15 cords of fire-wood. The salary was subsequently raised to £62, and fire-wood, and "a load of pine knots yearly to study by." After being relieved from preaching, his salary was reduced to £18 and 15 cords of fire-wood. One vote of the parish was, "the worthy Mr. McKinstry shall always be provided with a sufficiency of fire-wood." He continued the active pastor of the society until 1789, when he was released from preaching, but discharged other duties of the pastorate until his death.

Rev. Dr. Lathrop of West Springfield, in the sermon preached at his funeral thus described him :

"Mr. McKinstry was a man of good natural talents, a respectable scholar and sound divine. His preaching, though it suffered some disadvantage from the feebleness of his delivery, was edifying to his stated hearers. He was a man of exemplary piety, of a candid spirit, of a modest, humble disposition and of Christian fortitude and hope in view of approaching dissolution."

The parsonage house built in the early part of his ministry and occupied by him, was standing in 1858. The old edifice in which he preached has given place to a building more suited to modern taste, but is still standing and used for a barn.

In 1760, he married Eunice, a daughter of David Smith of Suffield, Conn., who died Sept. 4, 1820, aged 86. They had seven children, viz : *John Alexander*, b. Nov. 15, 1760 ; *Eunice Theodosia*, b. Dec. 20, 1762 ; *Elizabeth Lucy*, b. May 19, 1765 ; *Archibald*, b. Sept. 14, 1767 ; *Roger Augustus*, b. Dec. 28, 1769 ; *Perseus*, b. March 20, 1772 ; *Candace*, b. July 1, 1774. They all died at Chicopee, without issue, except Roger Augustus and Perseus, as follows, viz :

John Alexander, April 26, 1840.

Eunice T., Feb. 14, 1844.

.*Elizabeth L.*, May 19, 1826.

Archibald, a respected physician, Sept. 11, 1800.

Candace, the last survivor, Aug. 26, 1859, at the age of 85.

III. ROGER AUGUSTUS, son of John of Chicopee, was a tanner in Ashfield, then in Plainfield, Mass. About 1827, he removed to Geneva in Ohio, where he died Feb. 19, 1842. His wife was Chloe Elmer of Ashfield, by whom he had six children, viz :

IV. ¹ *Augustus*, died unmarried.

IV. ² *Orin*, b. April 1, 1776, married Maria Cook, and died without issue October 26, 1847 ; his wife died 1849.

IV. [3] *Eunice*, b. 1798, married Nahum Daniels and died without issue March 26, 1826.

IV. [4] *Lucina*, b. 1800, married in 1826 the same Daniels, by whom she has one son and one daughter, with whom she is living in Thompson. Her husband was drowned at Erie, Penn. in 1842.

IV. [5] *Archibald*, born Dec. 12, 1806, married Mary Silverthorn Dec. 21, 1831, and died April 16, 1862, in Geneva, Ohio. His children were, [1] Elmer Davis, b. Nov. 26, 1832, d. Oct. 18, 1834; [2] Lodeska H., d. Oct. 30, 1862; [3] Elmer D., b. Jan. 29, 1837, mar. in 1857; [4] Elizabeth J., b. Aug. 18, 1840; [5] Ella J., b. Sept. 19, 1845; [6] Stellenk, b. July 20, 1848; [7] Mary Adell, b. May 27, 1851; [8] Vernon, b. June 12, 1857.

IV. [6] *Lucy*, b. Jan. 12, 1808, mar. Dexter Ford, Jan. 11, 1828, and had a daughter Chlorinda, b. Nov., 1829, and two sons, Orin E. and Reuben D. b. in 1832 and 1833. Orin mar. in Dec. 1855. Ford d. March 14, 1836. She mar. 2nd, Nathaniel Millard, April 16, 1841, and is living with her husband and three children by him, viz., Nathaniel, Mary L. and Ida, in Wisconsin.

IV. [7] *Lyman*, died in 1822, aged 10 years.

Roger, the father, married a second wife who survived him, without issue.

III. PERSEUS, sixth child of Rev. John of Chicopee, b. 1772 d. in Chicopee, Aug. 23, 1829; was a tanner, first in Plainfield; then a farmer in Chicopee. Oct. 24, 1803, he mar. Grace, a daughter of Daniel Williams, of Norwich, Mass. She was born July 8, 1783 and died Dec. 24, 1855; they had eleven children, viz:

IV. [1] *Eliza*, b. Sept. 25, 1804, living on the homestead, unmarried.

IV. [2] *Emily*, b. April 8, 1806, mar. Dec. 16, 1830, Titus Chapin, a farmer in Chicopee, and died Oct. 14, 1842, leaving five children, viz: Titus, Roxana, Emily, Lucy and Eleonora, who was born in 1841, and died 1844. Her husband died in 1865. The son, [5] Titus, b. in 1831, was drowned at Topeka on Kanzas river, Aug. 14, 1858. [5] Roxana, while a teacher in Georgia, married General Wm. Gerdine, of Athens in that State, and had a son b. in 1859, and a daughter who died. [5] Emily, mar. Wm. D. Chapin, of Chicopee, Dec. 8, 1859, and had two children. Lucy died unmarried in 1862.

IV. [3] *Theodosia*, b. Aug. 23, 1807, mar. Whitman Chapin a farmer in Chicopee, Dec. 20, 1829, and had three children, viz: Moses Whitman, Harriet Eliza and Edward, and is living in Chicopee. Her husbandd. June 14, 1865. Her son Moses Whitman mar. Augusta Chapin, Oct. 26, 1853 and died Feb. 25, 1864, leaving children.

IV. ⁴ *William*, b. June 8, 1809 ; d. Feb. 24, 1845. He was a farmer in Chicopee ; he married Mary T. Frink and had two children, viz., Laura Jane, who married John White of Forrestville, N. Y. in 1856, and has one son and three daughters ; and Arthur, who was killed at the battle of Williamsburg May 5, 1862, at the age of 22. He was a young man of fine abilities and great promise. He was a nephew of Willard McKinstry, proprietor of the "Fre. donia Censor," and was a writer for that paper both poetry and prose, which were much commended. His letters from the army were valuable contributions to the literature of the war. He joined the army on the breaking out of the rebellion, although in feeble health, just rising from a bed of sickness.

The widow of William, IV. married for her second husband Austin Chapin and lives in Forrestville.

IV. ⁵ *John Alexander*, the 5th child of Perseus was b. April 19, 1811 : he graduated at Amherst College in 1838 ; pursued theological studies at the East Windsor Seminary ; licensed to preach by the Tolland Association Nov. 10, 1840 and settled as a Congregational minister, 1st in Torrington, Conn., in Oct. 1842, transferred to Harwinton in 1857. He closed his labors at that place in Oct. 1863, and is now preaching in Richfield, Ohio. In August, 1843, he married Mary E. Morton of Whately, Mass. and has three children, John Morton b. 1844, Wm. Alexander b. 1849, and Harriet Elvira b. Jan. 4, 1858.

IV. ⁶ *Willard*, b. April 9, 1813, died May 27, 1814.

IV. ⁷ *Willard*, b. May 9, 1815 ; he is publisher of the "Fredonia Censor," in Chatauque county, N. Y. and Postmaster of the town. In 1843, he mar. Maria A. Durlin, and has had four children, viz., Louis, Willard, Anna and Grace. Grace died in 1852: the others are living.

IV. ⁸ *Mary*, b. Nov. 2, 1817 ; mar. James B. Finch June 20, 1843, of Southampton, Mass. and has had six children, of whom two daughters are dead.

IV. ⁹ *Alfred*, b. May 17, 1821, d. 1823.

IV. ¹⁰ *Alfred Lyman*, b. April 20, 1823, mar. Jane Granger, June 2, 1852, and has two sons, Alfred and Wm. Edgar Granger, and one daughter, Mary Eliza.

IV. ¹¹ *Archibald Winthrop*, b. March 19, 1828 ; mar. Sept. 3, 1857, Helen E. daughter of N. B. Putnam, of Fredonia and has a son and daughter. He was associated until the present year with his brother Willard in the publication of the Fredonia Censor, but has now moved to Minnesota.

II. MARY, the second child of Rev. John of Ellington, b. Jan. 24, 1726, married Daniel Ellsworth, of Ellington, b. 1727, died July 27, 1803 ;

she died March 27, 1801. They had 10 children, viz , *Daniel*, died in infancy; *Daniel*, b. Dec. 3, 1758, married Mary Abbott Dec. 2, 1784, and d. March 3, 1798, a merchant in Erie, Penns., leaving issue. *Chloe*, mar. —— Hyde, of Norwich, Conn.; *Anna*, mar. —— Goodrich; *Lucretia*, married —— Little, of Ellington; *Mindwell, Alice* and *Betsey*, died unmarried. *John*, a missionary to the Isle of Sable, in the W. I., died without issue in 1791, aged 29; *Jerusha*, b. 1768, mar. Wm. Morgan, who died March 2, 1827, aged 59. She died April 29, 1820; they had 4 children, viz., William and Mary who died in childhood, 1814 and 1816; Lois mar. a gentleman of Texas, and died there, leaving one child who died soon after, and Alice who was a teacher in Kentucky before the war.

Daniel Ellsworth who married Mary McKinstry was a descendant of Josiah, an early settler of Windsor, the ancestor, also, of Chief Justice Oliver Ellsworth; the family were large proprietors in Ellington, which was formerly a part of Windsor. The houses of three brothers, Daniel, Charles and Gurdon, sons of Daniel, are standing on large farms near each other, venerable structures, about a mile and a half from the centre village. The children of Daniel III. and Mary (Abbott) Ellsworth were as follows, viz.:

IV. [1] *Betsey*, b. Dec. 24, 1785, d. July 24, 1797.

[2] *Mary*, b. Jan. 20, 1789, mar. Samuel Thompson, of Ellington, Nov. 9, 1809, and had 8 children, between Jan. 1811 and Aug., 1834, viz., V. [1] Philo E. b. Jan. 26, 1811, mar. Ellen C. Wallace, of New York, Sept. 30, 1838, and had 8 children, 4 sons and 4 daughters; he lives in Payson, Ill., his son David, graduated from Illinois College in 1862, and mar. Belle Faxon, of Payson, 1865. [2] Samuel, b. Aug. 13, 1813, died May 31, 1840. [3] Mary, b. April 18, 1816, mar. Oliver M. Hyde, of Ellington, Nov. 9, 1837, and has issue, a son and 2 daughters. [4] Emily, b. Dec. 20, 1818, lives in Ellington, unmarried. [5] Jane, b. Sept. 19, 1823, mar. Daniel N. Kimball, of Ellington, Jan. 20, 1848, and had 2 sons and 2 daughters; one daughter died in 1864, the eldest son d. in 1851. [6] Joseph Abbott. b. April 29, 1827, mar. Mabel Clark, of Enfield, Jan. 8, 1834, and has children. [7] Laura, b. July 17, 1829, d. Dec. 20, 1835. [8] Ellen, b. Aug. 20, 1834.

IV. [3] *Nancy*, third daughter of Daniel and Mary (Abbot) Ellsworth, b. Nov. 12, 1790, mar., 1st, Luther Scarborough, of West Hartford, in 1808, and had one daughter and 5 sons, all dead. 2nd, Wm. Wells, of Newtown, Ill., in 1843. She died Dec., 1843; her first husband died in 1820. Nancy's son, Daniel E., mar. in 1838, Mary W. Strong, and had 8 children.

IV. *John*, b. Aug. 22, 1792, mar. Hannah May, and lived in West Hartford; died Jan. 19, 1859, leaving issue. He had 7 children between 1839 and 1854.

IV.   *Sophia*, b. Aug. 13, 1794, mar. Deacon David Prince, of Brooklyn, Con., now of Payson, Ill., and died May 3, 1865. She had 6 children, 3 of each sex.

IV.   *Chloe*, b. March 18, 1796, died July 22, 1797.

II.   ALEXANDER, the third child of Rev. John, of Ellington, was b. May 16, 1728, and died in that town, Nov. 9, 1759. He married Sarah Lee, of Litchfield, Conn., and had three children, of whom *Ezekiel* alone, survived infancy ; his wife died Jan. 23, 1758, and his two children in 1750 and 1751.

III.   EZEKIEL, son of Alexander,[2] was born in Ellington, Aug. 17, 1753 and continued to reside on his father's homestead, until his death, Nov. 25, 1803. He married Rosina Chapman June 26, 1776. His widow, b. Feb. 10, 1758, d. April 24, 1839, aged 81. They had 12 children, viz.:

IV.   [1] *Sarah*, b. Nov. 8, 1777, married —— Ross, and d. Sept. 18, 1813, leaving 2 sons.

IV.   [2] *Elizabeth*, b. July 16, 1779, d. March 27, 1794.

IV.   [3] *Anna*, b. March 5, 1781, d. Dec. 6, 1798.

IV.   [4] *Rosina*, b. Jan. 25, 1783, mar. Leonard Dunton, who died in Rome, N. Y. She had 2 daughters, also dead. She died Sept., 1838.

IV.   [5] *Alexander*, b. April 9, 1785 ; he established himself as a merchant, in Augusta, Georgia, where he mar. Elizabeth, a daughter of Jesse Thompson, of that neighborhood, and a descendant of Gen. Elijah Clarke, a prominent citizen of that State, by whom he had one son, *Alexander*, and one daughter, *Ann*, who is living unmarried. He died in Charleston, S. C., Nov. 6, 1823; his widow mar. Dr. Henry Sullivan Lee, of Boston, son of Dr. Samuel Parsons Lee, of New York, and has by him 5 sons and 3 daughters. V. *Alexander*, son of Alexander,[4] b. at Augusta, Ga., March 7, 1822 ; he passed the early years of his life in New England. At the age of 13, he went to Mobile, Ala., and became a clerk in a commercial house; but having higher aspirations, he concluded to prepare for the bar, and entered the office of John A. Campbell, afterwards, Judge of the S. C. of the U. S., as a student ; was admitted to the bar in 1842 and had a successful practice. In 1850, he was elected Judge of the City Court of Mobile, having civil and criminal jurisdiction. During the rebellion, he became an officer in the Confederate service. In 1845, he married Virginia, a daughter of Robert R. Dale, by whom he has had three children, viz., Mary, Mordecai and William. He is an active member of the Methodist Episcopal church, and a man of integrity and ability.

IV. ⁶ *John*, b. June 16, 1787, died in Ellington, April 25. 1839, leaving
a widow and six children. His wife was Jerusha, daughter of
Lt. John McCray, of Ellington and Charlotte Wells; by whom
he had 7 sons and four daughters, viz. :
Charlotte, b. Nov. 28, 1816, married Edwin Reese of Alabama,
and has had 2 sons and 6 daughters.
² *Lee*, b. April 6, 1819, and lives in California, unmarried.
³ *Rosina*, b. March 16, 1821, married George Parnese and lives
in Washington, D. C.
⁴ *Fidelia*, b. March 22, 1823, mar. W. Summerfield Massie, July
29, 1848, and has 5 sons and 1 daughter.
⁵ *Jerusha*, b. April 7, 1825, mar. Israel P. Holton, of Galesboro', Ill.,
and has one son Frederick Arthur.
⁶ *Alexander*, b. Nov. 24, 1827, is living unmarried with his mother
on the homestead.
IV. ⁷ *Fanny*, b. April 6, 1789 ; d. unmarried, Jan. 27, 1809.
IV. ⁸ *Oliver*, b. July 14, 1791, was a physician in Monson, Mass., where
he died in March, 1852, the last survivor of Ezekiel's children.
By his wife, Matilda Spaulding, he had two sons and three
daughters ; one of the sons died in 1835, aged 23 ; the other is
a physician in Alden, New York ; the daughters are unmarried.
IV. ⁹ *Lee*, b. March 8, 1793, d. May 29, 1808.
IV. ¹⁰ *Elizabeth*, b. May 26, 1795, mar. Augustus Pease, a merchant.
in Hartford, Conn., by whom she had three sons and one daughter who mar. Mr. Dutton, of Rochester, N. Y. One son is
dead ; the others, Claudius and Julius, married and were living
in New York in 1858.
IV. ¹¹ *Jerusha*, b. Jan. 8, 1798 ; d. Sept. 13, 1801.
IV. ¹² *Anna*, b. Aug. 16, 1800 ; mar. Benjamin P. Johnson, then a
lawyer in Rome, N. Y., afterwards of Albany. She died Jan.
28, 1837, leaving two sons and three daughters. One son,
Alexander, mar. and lived in Chicago in 1858, having had one
son ; another son, Edward Kirk, was at that time living with
his father in Albany. One daughter, Rose, mar. H. B. Woodbridge and lived in Galesboro', Ill.

II. WILLIAM, the third son and fourth child of John of Ellington,
was born Oct. 8, 1732. He was a physician, and settled in Taunton,
Mass. prior to 1759. On Nov. 27, 1760, he married Priscilla, daughter
of the Rev. Nathaniel Leonard, pastor of the 1st Church in Plymouth,
Mass., and Priscilla, daughter of Nathaniel Rogers and Sarah Appleton
of Ipswich, Mass. By her he had ten children, viz : ¹ *William*, b. Nov.
13, 1762; he graduated at Oxford University, Eng.; became Rector of
East Grinstead and Lingfield, near London ; was tutor to children of

several noblemen, whom he accompanied in their travels on the continent. He was a good scholar and a polished gentleman, and died on a visit to this country, unmarried, in August, 1823. [2] *Priscilla*, b Aug. 25, 1765; married John Hazen, of New Brunswick, and had a large family. [3] *Sarah*, b. Aug. 14, 1767; married Major Caleb Stark, son of Gen. John Stark, and had a numerous family. [4] *John*, b. March 6, 1769, a merchant in Boston several years; died, unmarried, Oct. 29, 1825. [5] *Mary* and [6] *Thomas*, twins, b. Aug. 17, 1770. Thomas d. unmarried in 1796. Mary married Benjamin Willis, of Haverhill, Portland and Boston, Jan. 9, 1791, and had eight children. [7] *Elizabeth*, b. Oct. 26, 1762; married to Samuel Sparhawk, of Portsmouth and Concord, N. H., Secretary of that State in 1803, by whom she had several children. [8] *David*, b. 1775, and d. unmarried in New York, a merchant, in March, 1800.

They had two other children, viz: William, born and died Nov. 13, 1761; and John, b. Nov. 3, 1764, died Dec. 21, 1768, in the 5th year of his age. All in Taunton.

Dr. McKinstry had a successful business in Taunton, in 1774, although he had a feeble constitution and a consumptive habit. The Rev. Mr. Emery, in his "Ministry of Taunton," says of Dr. McKinstry, "He was a person of highly respectable personal and professional character." At that time a Capt. Gilbert, suspected of tory principles, was seized and so roughly handled by the "sons of liberty," that it became necessary to have a surgeon to dress his wounds. He protested against having a rebel doctor, but was willing that Dr. McKinstry should attend him. This suggestion excited suspicion against this amiable and popular physician. He became the subject of offensive remark, and was exposed to insult and injury. Being in feeble health and of a sensitive nature, which could not bear hard usage nor a suspected position, he thought it advisable to retire for a time to Boston. His family, which was left in Taunton, was now subject to increased annoyance. His wife, a finely educated and high spirited woman, of elegant manners, was treated with much harshness as a suspected person. She was niece of the Hon. George Leonard, of Norton, and cousin of Daniel Leonard, a refugee, and afterwards chief Justice of Bermuda.

Mrs. McKinstry with her family soon joined her husband in Boston. So high was Dr. McKinstry's reputation in his profession, that he received from Gen. Gage the appointment of surgeon general of the hospitals in Boston. His property in Taunton was confiscated.

It so happened that on the memorable 17th of June, 1775, a dinner party took place at Dr. McKinstry's house, for which invitations had been given out the day before. The dinner proved to be a solemn and silent one, and was partaken standing. Several officers were present who had been detailed to proceed with detachments of the British army to dislodge the rebels from Bunker Hill. They hastily dined and proceeded to join their corps ; among them was Major John Small, a friend of the family whose name is identified with that momentous battle. Dr. McKinstry's house stood on Hanover street, near where the Shawmut House lately stood, and the children went to the top of the house to witness the cannonade. Sarah, one of them, then eight years old, little dreamed that, in after years, she would become the wife of a gallant stripling of 16, who was then fighting in the opposing ranks, by the side of his veteran father, the renowned John Stark. Twelve years after, she was wedded to that gallant soldier, Caleb Stark. Another daughter, Mary, might also have been a distant witness to the flight from the flames of Charlestown of her future husband, Benjamin Willis, a native of that devoted town, who, with his mother, was compelled to make a hasty retreat, without a backward look to their perishing property.

When Boston was evacuated, Dr. McKinstry and his family went on board the fleet, which lay ten days in Nantasket Roads waiting orders. During that time, viz., March 21, 1776, Dr. McKinstry died of consumption, on board the Dutton hospital ship at the age of 43 years, and his remains lie buried on George's Island, in that harbor.

The surviving members of the family were taken in the fleet to Halifax, and were on board the same ship with lady Howe, wife of the Admiral, where they were treated with that sympathy and kindness their unhappy condition required. The fleet took away about one thousand refugees. The family remained in Halifax, with the exception of William, the eldest son, until 1778, when they returned to the States, making Newport, R. I., their place of residence, during its occupation by the British. After its evacuation, in Nov., 1779. they proceeded to Haverhill, in Mass., where a sister of Mrs. McKinstry, the wife of John White, Esq., lived ; and she died there, May 26, 1786, honored and loved.

The four sons of Dr. McKinstry died unmarried, and consequently the *name* in this branch is extinct.

Rev. *William*,[3] died at Concord, N. H., Aug. 26, 1823, aged 61.

John,[3] died in Ohio, Oct. 29, 1825, aged 56 years.

Thomas.[3] died at sea, 1796, aged 26, the vessel never heard from.

David,[3] died in New York, March 3, 1800, of consumption, aged 27.

III. The Rev. WILLIAM McKINSTRY,.[3] son of Dr. William,[2] entered the naval service of Great Britain at the commencement of the revolution. In an engagement with an American privateer, in 1776, he lost his right hand and was shot overboard. He contrived to keep himself above water until the battle was over, when he was relieved from his critical situation. This changed the current of his life, and instead of becoming a naval officer, he became an episcopal clergyman, a cultivated scholar, and a gentleman of refined manners. He happened to be on the continent, and at a hotel in Munich, when Gen. Moreau arrived at the same hotel, in a most unpretending style, to take charge of the French army in that neighborhood. In a few days after, was fought the celebrated battle of Hohenlinden, and Mr. McKinstry, with the poet Thomas Campbell, had the good fortune to be near the scene of the combat; a cannon ball struck near the spot where they were standing, which rather discomposed the nerves of the poet. Mr. McKinstry had seen the article before. Campbell's immortal poem, written soon after, commemorates this most bloody passage of arms.

A gentleman who knew him personally writes to me as follows, " He was a noble specimen of humanity, and would have commanded respect in any situation in life. He was generous, affable and dignified, and possessed of more than ordinary talents." I have a MS. sermon written by him with his left hand, which is very distinct and well written.

We will dispose of this branch of the family by a brief notice of descendants in the female line, all of whom married and left children.

III.   PRISCILLA, the eldest daughter of Dr. McKinstry, married at Haverhill, Mass. John Hazen, Sept. 2, 1787. Mr. Hazen descended from Edward Hazen who came from England prior to 1650 and settled in Rowley, through Richard, Moses and John. His parents were John Hazen and Ann Sweat. He was nephew of General Hazen of N. H., who served in the French war, and also with reputation in the war of the revolution; he died without issue in New York, in 1802. The nephew, after his marriage, established himself on a large and valuable farm in Burton, at the junction of the Oromucto river with the St. John, in New Brunswick, where he died. They had twelve children, as follows:

IV. [1] *Eliza*, b. July 14, 1778, mar. Samuel A. Kimball, a lawyer in Concord, N. H. and had a large family of children. He died in 1856, and she a few years later.

IV. [2] *William McKinstry*, b. April 26, 1790, died July, 1859.

IV. [3] *George Leonard*, } b. July 16, 1792. George died unmarried.
IV. [4] *John*, twins,

John mar. a Scotch lady by whom he had one son, who is living with his mother at Burton. John had a commission in the English army and was afterwards Sheriff of the county.

IV. [5] *Charles*, b. June 10, 1794, mar. Mary a daughter of Simeon Jones, a refugee from Weston, Mass., and has had two daughters, one mar. James White, Sheriff of Sunbury county, N. B., the other Elizabeth, mar. Alexander Gilmore, of Calais, Me. Charles occupies his father's homestead at Burton.

IV. [6] *Mary Ann*, b. June 1, 1796, mar. George Gerdine, and died April, 1846, leaving children.

IV. [7] *James*, b. March 9, 1798, d. unmarried 1856.

IV. [8] *Robert*, b. March 28, 1800, d. leaving two children.

IV. [9] *Thomas*, b. Jan. 4, 1802, was a merchant, and died unmarried at Metamoras, in Mexico, 1847.

IV. [10] *Sarah*, b. March 16, 1804, d. unmarried in 1863

IV. [11] *Charlotte*, b. April 26, 1806, mar. Mr. Hubbard, of Burton ; has no children.

IV. [12] *Nathaniel Merrill*, b. April 21, 1808, d. unmarried in California.

Mrs. Hazen died in New Brunswick in March, 1827, and he several years before.

III. SARAH, the 2nd daughter of Dr. McKinstry,[2] married Major Caleb Stark, in Haverhill, in 1787. Major Stark was the eldest son of Gen. John Stark, of revolutionary fame, and was born Dec. 3, 1759. He accompanied his father as a volunteer, and was present at the battle of Bunker Hill ; soon after was appointed Ensign in Capt. George Reid's company, in the 1st N. H. Regiment. He served in New York and Canada ; he was an adjutant in the battles of Trenton and Princeton ; was present at the battle of Saratoga, and Springfield, N. J.; served as adjutant general of the Northern Department, in 1778 and 1781, and continued in service to the close of the war. After the peace he engaged in mercantile pursuits ; was awhile established in Boston with his brother-in-law, John McKinstry, and engaged in manufacturing at Pembroke, N. H. He was a man of great courage, energy, and perseverance through life. He died in Ohio, Aug. 26, 1838, where he had proceeded to establish a claim to land granted for military services. The principal residence of his family was a fine seat in Dunbarton, N. H., which still belongs to the family, and is their summer resort.

Mrs. Stark died Sept. 11, 1839, aged 72. Their children were :

IV. [1] *John William*, b. Oct. 24, 1788. Sometime a resident in Calcutta (India), afterwards a merchant in Boston ; d. unmarried, Jan. 6, 1836.

IV. [2] *Harriet*, ⎫ twins—b. in 1790. Sarah died in infancy ; Harriet is
  [3] *Sarah*, ⎭ living on the paternal estate at Dunbarton, N. H.

IV. [4] *Elizabeth*, b. 1792, mar. Samuel Newell, a merchant of Boston, by whom she had several children, and is living a widow in New York. Her son Samuel took the name of John Stark, and d. May 11, 1849, leaving children.

IV. [5] *Charles*, ⎫ b. 1794. Charles d. unmarried Nov. 5, 1815 ;
  [6] *Sarah*, twins, ⎭ Sarah mar. Joshua Winslow, a merchant in Boston, and are both dead, leaving one son, the late Commander Winslow, of the Navy, who died at sea in the service, Aug. 23, 1862. He was born Sept. 6, 1818 : entered the Navy a Midshipman 1833, and made his first cruise in the Brandywine. Nov. 24, 1844, he was appointed Lieut., afterwards promoted to the rank of Commander and was Flag Officer under Com.

Long, on the Pacific station. When the war broke out he was ordered to the Mississippi steam frigate; soon after, transferred to the R. R. Cuyler, in which he captured the rebel schr. Wilder under a heavy fire, on the coast of Florida. He was on a cruise, three days out of Key West, when he died of yellow fever: a brave, accomplished and beloved officer. He left a widow and children.

IV. [7] *Henry*, b. 1796, mar. Emma Beverly Randolph, of Maryland, whose mother was a daughter of Gen. Lingard, of Baltimore; he died in Maryland in 1865, without issue.

IV. [8] *Mary Ann*, b. 1798, d. unmarried May 12, 1815.

IV. [9] *Charlotte*, b. 1803, living at Dunbarton, unmarried.

IV. [10] *Caleb*, b. 1803, grad. at H. C. in 1823, was a lawyer, and an historical writer of distinction in N. H. He died at Dunbarton, unmarried, in 1864. He published a life of his grand-father John Stark, the hero of Bennington, and memoirs of his father also a history of Dunbarton, and other papers.

IV. [11] *David McKinstry*, b. 1806, d. unmarried Oct. 26, 1832.

None of this family left issue but Elizabeth and Sarah.

III. MARY, the third daughter of Dr. McKinstry,[2] married Benjamin Willis, January 9, 1791. He was the eldest son of Benjamin Willis, who was born in Boston, 1743, only son of Benjamin Willis, of that town, who died in 1745. Mr. Willis was born in Charlestown, March 5, 1768, then lived in Haverhill, to which place his family had fled from the flames of Charlestown, where they then resided, June 17, 1775. He moved to Portland, Me., in 1803, and to Boston in 1815. His wife died in Boston, Feb. 12, 1847, after a union of fifty-six years; he died Oct. 1, 1853, aged 85 years and over 7 months. They had eight children, viz:

IV. [1] BENJAMIN, born at Haverhill, Nov. 16, 1791.
    [2] WILLIAM,   "   "   "   Aug. 31, 1794.
    [3] GEORGE,   "   "   "   June 16, 1797, d. Oct. 24, 1844.
    [4] THOMAS,   "   "   "   Mar. 15, 1800, d. July, 1814, unm.
    [5] HENRY,   "   "   "   April 13, 1802.
    [6] MARY,   "   " Portland, Dec. 14, 1805.
    [7] ELIZABETH, "   "   "   Oct. 25, 1807, d. May 3, 1856.
    [8] THOMAS LEONARD, b. at Portland, Apr. 4, 1812, d. Sept. 13, 1845.

IV. *Benjamin* [1] was a merchant in Portland, Me., many years, moved to Boston and retired on a competency. He married Elizabeth Sewall, a daughter of Col. Joseph May, of Boston, Sept. 19, 1817. She died in 1822, leaving two children, *Hamilton*, b. in 1818, and *Elizabeth*, b. Sept. 12, 1820. Hamilton mar. 1st, Louisa, a daughter of Dr. Winship, of Roxbury, who, dying in 1862 without issue, he married in 1863 Helen Phillips, daughter of Samuel Phillips, and has in 1865, one child. Elizabeth, in 1838, mar. Thomas G. Wells, of Boston, and had 2 sons and 3 daughters, all unmarried. Her oldest son, Henry, was an officer in the Navy, of great promise, and was lost at sea in 1864, in command of an armed vessel. They live with her father in Brookline, Mass.

IV. *William,*[2] graduated at Harvard College in 1813, was admitted to the Suffolk Bar, Boston, in Jan., 1817 ; removed to Portland in 1819, where he is still in the practise of his profession; was State Senator in 1855, Mayor of Portland in 1857; Elector of President of U. S. in 1860; President of the Maine Historical Society 1856 to 1864, and author of the History of Portland, the Law and Lawyers of Maine, and several other works. Sept., 1, 1823, he mar. Julia a daughter of Ezekiel Whitman, late Chief Justice of the Supreme Court of Maine, by whom he had eight children, two only surviving in 1865, viz., Julia the wife of Dr. Barron C . Watson, now in Europe, by whom she has two sons living; and Henry, b. 1831, mar. to Adeline Fitch in 1855, and has one daughter b. 1857. He graduated at Bowdoin College 1851, and Harvard Law School 1854.

IV. *George,*[3] late a merchant in Portland, Me. ; married, 1st, Caroline, daughter of Col. Richard Hunnewell, by whom he had one child, which died in infancy. 2d, Clarissa May, daughter of Caleb B. Hall, Esq., a native of Medford, Mass., by whom he had nine children ; three sons, George H., Benjamin W., and Caleb Hall, with four daughters, survive. He died Oct. 24, 1844. Two sons are unmarried ; George, his eldest son, b. June 28, 1825, mar. in 1863, Harriet, a daughter of Thomas Hammond, Jr., of Portland and has one child. The four daughters married and have issue : Mary to George Wyer, Caroline to Mr. Lyman of New York, Charlotte to Lewellyn True, who is dead, and Ann to Samuel B. Parris, of Washington.

IV. *Henry,*[5] a retired merchant ; resides in Roxbury, Mass., unmarried. He represented that city in the legislature in 1858.

IV. *Mary,*[6] married James H. Duncan of Haverhill, Mass., June 28, 1826, a graduate of Harvard College in 1812. By him she has had thirteen children, seven of whom are living, viz., two sons, Samuel W., b. 1838, a graduate of Brown University in 1860, and George W., b. 1846. Two of the daughters are married, viz., Mary, in 1857, to Mr. Harris of Chicago, and Elizabeth to the Rev. Theodore T. Munger of Haverhill, in 1864 ; they have no issue. The other children, viz., Rebecca W., Caroline and Margaret, remain unmarried. Mr. Duncan was born in Haverhill, Dec. 5, 1793, son of James Duncan, a descendant of the

Scotch-Irish stock of Londonderry. He has been a member of the Governor's Council, and twice represented his District in Congress, and held other important official stations. He is by profession a lawyer. His eldest son James H. was a graduate of Brown University in the class of 1848, was a merchant in Haverhill at the time of his death. Samuel entered the army as a volunteer Captain, and was at the siege and capture of Vicksburg, and afterwards studied divinity.

IV. *Elizabeth,[7]* married Henry W. Kinsman of Newburyport, son of Dr. Aaron Kinsman of Portland, who graduated at Dartmouth College [in 1787, and Ann Willis, sister of Benjamin, Oct. 1, 1828. Mr. Kinsman was born in Portland, March 6, 1803; graduated at Dartmouth College in 1822, and was connected in law business with Daniel Webster, in Boston, prior to his moving to Newburyport. He has represented his State in the Senate and House of Representatives of Massachusetts, and was Collector of the Customs in Newburyport under President Harrison. By his wife he had eleven children; three daughters only survive. His wife died May 6, 1856, aged 49, and he mar., 2d, Martha F., daughter of John Titcomb of Newburyport, Oct. 5, 1858, who survives him without children. He died Dec. 4, 1859. His daughter Clara C., b. 1836, married Gamaliel Bradford of Boston, Oct. 30, 1861, and the next, Mary McKinstry, b. Mar. 10, 1839, married James M. Howe of Boston in 1862; both have children. Louisa H., the youngest child, b. Nov. 12, 1849, is unmarried. None of the other children were married.

IV. *Thomas Leonard,[8]* a merchant, afterwards farmer in Illinois; married Charlotte Elizabeth, daughter of Caleb B. Hall, of Bucksport, Oct. 11, 1832. They had six children, two only survive, one daughter and one son, Thomas L. born Nov. 25, 1841; the daughter, Ellen M., born in Portland, June 21, 1835; married Sept. 7, 1851, Joseph A. Ware, a lawyer of Portland, son of Judge Ashur Ware, and has one son; they live in Washington, D. C. The other daughter, Emily, b. June 13, 1837, married Lewis Pierce, a lawyer in Portland, June 13, 1860, and d. in October, 1864, leaving two daughters and a son. He died Sept. 13, 1845, aged 33.

III. ELIZABETH, the fourth and-youngest daughter of Dr. William McKinstry,[2] born Oct. 26, 1772, was married to Samuel Sparhawk of Portsmouth, N. H., in 1803. Mr. Sparhawk was a man of fine family, was connected with the Hon. Nathaniel Sparhawk of New Hampshire, and himself held many offices in his native State, of honor and trust. He was Secretary of State for N. H. from 1810 to 1814 and from 1816 to

1825. He died in Conway, N. H., Nov. 22, 1834, a man of unimpeach-able integrity and honor. They had but three children.

IV. [1] *Oliver*, married, and died without issue.

   [2] *Thomas.*

   [3] *Elizabeth*, married Edward Winslow, son of Issac Winslow of Boston, and has no children.

IV. *Thomas* resides in Amesbury, Mass.; married Miss Renton, a Scotch lady, and has children. He is a physician, skilful, in good practice, and highly esteemed.

II. PAUL, the fifth child and youngest son of the Rev. John[1] of Ellington, born Sept. 17, 1734, died June 14, 1818. He had three wives. By the 1st, Sarah Laird, of Stafford, Conn., he had six children born in Ellington, viz., *Alexander*, *Salmon*,[2] *Alvin*,[3] *Elizabeth*,[4] *Alice*,[5] *Polly*[6]. By his second wife, Widow Abigail Stone, whose maiden name was Dean, and who had five children by Stone, he had two children, *Sarah*[7] and *William*,[8] who were born in Bethel, Vermont, to which place their parents had moved. By his 3d wife he had no children. His first wife died Aug. 5, 1778, aged 36.

III. [1] *Alexander*, his eldest son, was born Dec. 10, 1762, and died in Vermont, Feb. 11, 1817. He married, 1st, Abigail, daughter of Thomas Cooper, who died April 8, 1804: by her he had four daughters and one son, viz., *Betsey*, b. Jan. 10 1794; *Pluma*, b. July 22, 1795; *Alice*, b. Aug. 13, 1797; *Sophronia* b. May 6, 1801, and *Alexander*, b. July 1, 1803. His 2d wife was Joiner, by whom he had 2 children, *Polly* b. Aug. 1 and *Abigail*, b. Sept. 24, 1816. The daughters all married, viz., Betsey to Solomon Walbridge, a farmer and had four children; Pluma, 1st to Gardner Paige and had five children. 2d to Richard Rawson, Jr. and had one son, who died young. Alice to Samuel Adams and had 3 daughters. Sophronia to Lucius B. Babbitt and had 2 daughters and 1 son, Polly to Udney Burk in 1835, and had 2 daughters and 1 son; Abigail to Timothy Pearl in 1832, and had 3 daughters. The eldest son, Alexander,[4] was a tallow chandler in Syracuse, of which city he has been Mayor. He married Sarah Clark in 1834, and had 3 sons, William, Alexander and Charles Henry, and 1 daughter, Helen Florence. His wife died in 1857. William is married and lives in Syra-cuse, as does Charles. Alexander entered the army in 1862, served through the war; was often wounded and retired with the rank of Captain.

III. [2] *Salmon*, b. Oct. 19, 1766, married Jerusha Baldwin Jan. 27, 1795, by whom he had 12 children; 5 sons, *Eleazer*, *Ezekiel*, *Salmon*, *John W.*, and *Clark*, and 7 daughters, all born between

Dec. 4, 1795 and Nov. 7, 1821 ; all but 2 daughters had families, He lived in Stafford, Conn., where he died Nov. 1, 1853. Eleazer mar. and had 3 sons and 6 daughters, Ezekiel had 3 children, John had 3 children, Clark had 5 children. Polly had 6 children, Nancy mar. Holmes of Stafford and had 4 children, Abigail had 10 children, Eveline, 1 child, Luria d. young, and 2 are unmarried.

III. ³ *Alvin*, b. July 13, 1769, married Widow Hannah (Baldwin) Russell, and lived in Bethel, Vt., where he died Oct. 3, 1853. He had 3 children ; 2 daughters, *Lucetta* and *Emily*, and 1 son, *Paul.* Lucetta b. June 7, 1805, married Edward Morris of Bethel, and died May 29, 1829, without issue : Paul b. July 17, 1807, married Harriet Lillie, of Bethel, and had 3 sons and 5 daughters, Alvin was the oldest son. Emily b. Nov 13, 1809 ; married Simeon A. Babbitt, of Randolph. Vt., and had 7 children,—4 daughters and 3 sons, viz., Robert A., Elbridge H., George A. Jeannette, the oldest child, Emily Jane, Mary L. and Lizzie A.

III. ⁴ *Elizabeth*, b. Nov. 28, 1771, married Samuel Loomis and had seven children, viz., *Samuel, Eliza, Alvin, Almerian, Miranda, Sarah* and *Maria.* She died in Middletown, Conn., May 10, 1847, aged 75. Alvin d. in Barre, April 17, 1804, aged 42 ; Almerian d. in New Orleans, Sept., 1842; Samuel d. April 19, 1828, aged 31 ; Miranda d. Oct. 11, 1818, aged 18.

III. ⁵ *Alice*, b. Aug. 17, 1774, married Othniel Eddy. of Vermont, and had 9 children, 3 sons and 6 daughters, viz., *Moore*, b. Jan. 15, 1795, married, his family live in Ohio. *Sarah*, b. 1798, married —— Webster, is a widow with family in Stafford, Conn. *Ruby*, b. 1800, married —— Wasson ; is a widow in Albany, N. Y., without issue. *Clarissa*, b. 1802, married James D. Wasson, of Albany, N. Y., and has a family. *Hiram*, b. 1805, died 1806. *Emily*, b. 1807, died same year. *John Randolph*, b. 1809, married and lives in Ohio with a family. *Almira* and *Elvira*, twins, b. 1813, d. in 1814.

III. ⁶ *Polly*, b. 1776, died 1778.

III. ⁷ *Sarah*, b. 1783, married Joel Eddy, brother of Othniel, and had 7 sons and 2 daughters. She died in Randolph, Vt., Sept. 28, 1834. Her children were *Hiram*, b. 1806. *William*, b. 1808, *Abigail*, b. 1808, twins,—she died 1837. *Philander*, b. 1810. *Harry*, b. 1812, d. 1841. *Harriet*, b. 1812, d. 1813. *Charles*, b. 1815. *McKinstry*, b. 1821, *Martin S.*, b. 1826. Hiram is a farmer in Redford, N. Y. William and Charles are Iron found. ers in Troy, N. Y., and William a merchant in the same place. Philander lives in Chicago, and McKinstry in Randolph.

III. [5] *William*, b. May 19, 1784. He is living in retirement on a competency acquired by prudence and industry, in Middletown, Conn., and is the last of the *grand-children* of the Rev. John, the first of the name who came to this country. He has a deep veneration for his ancestors and a warm sympathy for his kindred. In 1859, he erected a handsome granite monument over the graves of his grand-parents in the ancient cemetery at Ellington, on the marble tablet of which are inscribed appropriate memorials.

Sept. 2, 1821, he married Harriet M., a daughter of Phineas Dean, of Chatham, now Portland, in Conn., who died there June 29, 1833. Mrs. Wm. McKinstry was descended from Jonathan Dean and Sarah Clark, of Plainfield, Conn., through her grand-father, Phineas, b. July 19, 1710, and her father Phineas, b. Jan. 4, 1758; her mother was Ruth Hall. She was b. Sept. 14, 1801. They have no children. They adopted a relative who married Charles Chapman in 1861, and died in 1864, without issue.

Another branch of the McKinstry family came to this country. Tradition and circumstances furnish strong evidence of a common origin with the branch I have been describing, and I conjecture that they descended either from a brother or son of Rodger. The first comer of this family was—

I. Capt. JOHN McKINSTRY, who was born in Armagh, in the Province of Ulster, Ireland, in 1712. He married in Ireland, Jane Dickie, widow of ——— Belknap, of the County of Antrim. He came to this country about 1740; remained near Boston awhile, then went to Londonderry, in New Hampshire, where his first son, *John*, was born, 1745. His other children were, *Thomas, David, Charles* and *Sarah*. Sarah, b. 1754; married Dr. Bird, of Hillsdale, N Y., and had two daughters, Nancy and Hannah. She died in 1780, aged 26. Mrs McKinstry (Belknap) had one son by her first husband, who was an officer in the British army, and was in the service at New York, at the time of the revolution. A meeting was concerted between him and his brother-in-law, John McKinstry, about the time the British were evacuating New York, but it failed by the fleet's sailing before his brother reached the place of appointment. They were officers in the opposing forces. Capt. McKinstry also had been an officer in the English army; he died at Hillsdale, Columbia Co., N. Y., Oct. 6, 1776, aged 64.

II. JOHN, son of Capt. John,[1] b. in Londonderry, N. H., 1745; married Elizabeth Knox, of Rumford, Conn., by whom he had eight sons and three daughters, viz:

III. [1] *James*, b in Blandford, Mass., May 2, 1767; d. April 1, 1768.

III. [2] *Rachel*, b. March 16, 1769; married Sturgeon Sloan, an American officer, and died without issue, May 16, 1855.

III. [2] *George*, b. at Hillsdale, Jan. 20, 1772; living with a family, in Hudson, N. Y., 1858.

III. [4] *Elizabeth*, b. at Hillsdale, Nov. 24, 1774; married Walter T. Livingston and had issue; she d. Nov. 13, 1841.

III. [5] *John*, b. at Hillsdale, Aug. 5, 1777; married and had issue; d. Sept. 30, 1846.

III. [6] *William*, b. at Hillsdale, Dec. 25, 1779; married and had issue; d. Dec. 2. 1829.

III [7] *Henry*, b. at Hillsdale, Oct. 10, 1782; married and living in Hudson.

III. [8] *Sarah*, b. at Hudson, April 5, 1785; died Oct. 31, 1786.

III. [9] *Ansel*, b. at Hudson, Sept. 30, 1787; living at Hudson, 1858.

III. [10] *Nathaniel Green*, b. at Hillsdale, April 23, 1791; d. Sept. 4, 1794.

III. [11] *Robert*, b. at Livingston, Oct. 19, 1794; living at Hudson, 1858.

John, II., saw some service in the French war, though young; and at the commencement of the revolution joined the American army; was at the battle of Bunker Hill and the principal northern battles. He was taken prisoner at "the Cedars," in Canada, and came near losing his life to gratify savage revenge. He was bound to a stake and the faggots piled around him; when, it occurring to him that the Indian chief, Brandt, was a mason, he communicated to him the masonic sign, which caused his immediate release and subsequent good treatment. He was afterwards promoted to a colonelcy in a New York regiment, and served during the war. He died at Livingston, June 9, 1822; his widow, April 7, 1833.

II. THOMAS, son of Capt. John,[1] married, 1st, Elizabeth Green, by whom he had *Nancy* and *Thomas*. By his 2d wife, he had *Sarah*, 1782, died 1851; *Hollis* died in Greenport, N. Y., unmarried, 1858, and *Orenzo*. Hollis was the last surviving member of this family.

II. DAVID, son of John,[1] married Martha Cauley, by whom he had two sons, Charles and David; and four daughters, Mary, Susan, Clarissa and Sarah.

II. CHARLES, son of John,[1] born at Blandford, 1755; mar. Tabitha Patterson, at Hillsdale, where he was living in 1774; she died 1787, aged 32. In 1790, he married Nancy Norton, of Farmington, who died May 24, 1798, aged 35. He died at Hillsdale, Dec. 31, 1819, aged 64. By his first wife, he had—

III. [1] *Jane*, married Asahel Porter, 1796, and had one son, Thomas, born 1798. They all died in Greenfield, N. Y.

III. [2] *David Charles*, b. Aug. 12, 1778; married and died at Ypsilanti, in Michigan, Sept. 9, 1856, leaving issue, as hereinafter stated.

III. ³ *Sally*, b. Aug. 13, 1780 ; died at Hillsdale, April 17, 1845 ; married Augustus Tremain, 1798, and had issue, Charles Patter son, d. 1834, Augustus Porter, and Jane.

III. ⁴ *Oliver*, b. June 9, 1783 ; d. 1788.

III. ⁵ *Justus*, b. Oct. 27, 1785 ; died at the Astor House, N Y., May 21, 1849. ⁶ Daughter, died at birth, 1787.

By second wife, Nancy Norton, he had—

III. ⁷ *Charles Norton*, b. Jan. 16, 1792 ; d. at Hillsdale, 1794.

III. ⁸ *Melinda*, b. June 12, 1794 ; married Henry Loop, of Hempstead, L. I., 1829, and has one son, Charles Norton Loop, a merchant in New York. She is the only survivor of the children, and was living in Hempstead, 1858.

III. ⁹ *Nancy*, b. July 28, 1796 ; married Bowen Whiting, Sept. 18, 1819, by whom she had one son, John Nicols, b. at Geneva, 1821, and is a lawyer in New York. She died at Geneva, July 24, 1847, and her husband, at the same place, Dec. 1849.

III. ¹⁰ *Marianne*, b. May 16, 1798 ; d. May 24, 1798.

His 3d wife, whom he married at Great Barrington, Jan. 18, 1803, was Bernice Egliston, who died April 2, 1845, aged 76,—by her he had,

¹¹ *Edward Whiting*, b. June 24, 1804 ; d. April 9, 1805.

¹² *Edwin*, b. Nov. 10, 1805 ; died at Metamoras, March 9, 1849.

I add to what I have said above of the children of *Charles*, the son of John (I), the following particulars.

III. DAVID CHARLES, his 2d child, married Nancy Whiting Backus, 1805, who is now living at Ypsilanti ; their children were—

IV. ¹ *James Paterson*, b. at Hillsdale, 1807, Captain in U. S. N. ; married Jan. 23, 1858, Mary W. Smart, daughter of the late Gen. J. R. Williams, of Detroit. He entered the service Feb. 1, 1826 ; his sea service is near 20 years. Appointed Captain July 16, 1861. He was severely wounded in passing the rebel batteries near Port Hudson in 1863, from which he has not entirely recovered. In 1865, he was in command of the Receiving ship in New York harbor.

IT. ² *Sarah Ingersoll*, b. 1809 ; living in Ypsilanti.

IV. ³ *Augustus Tremain*, b. 1811 ; died at Ypsilanti, April 24, 1858.

IV. ⁴ *Justus*, b. at Hudson, 1814 ; grad. at West Point, 1838 ; married Susan McKinstry, daughter of George McKinstry (III.), 1838, and has three sons living,—Charles Frederick, James H., and Carlisle P. He was General in the U. S. Army until 1862. He served through the Seminole war in Florida, and through the Mexican war under Gen. Scott, and was brevetted several times [for distinguished services. On the breaking out of the rebellion, he was sent to St. Louis as Quarter Master, and at the request of Gen. Fremont, appointed a General Officer and took command.

But falling under the displeasure of the enemies of his friend, Gen. Fremont, he became their victim. He is now in civil life in New York.

IV. [5] *Ann*, b. at Detroit, 1817; married Houston Van Clive, 1849, and has one daughter, Margaretta, and is living at Ann Harbor, Michigan.

IV. [6] *Charles*, b. at Detroit, 1819; graduated at New Brunswick 1843, and was a lawyer in New York; died June 23, 1855.

IV. [7] *Elisha Williams*, b at Detroit, 1824. Judge of Supreme Court in California.

III. GEORGE, 3d child of Col. John,[2] b. 1772; married Susan Hamilton, daughter of Patrick Hamilton, M. D., of Canaan, N. Y.; she died in Hudson, N. Y., May 4, 1862. Their children were—

IV. [1] *Eliza*, b. in Canaan, Aug. 17, 1802; d. Feb. 1, 1804.

IV. [2] *Alexander H.*, born in Athens, N. Y., Feb. 17, 1805; mar. Angelina Pease, and had five children, viz., [1] Elisha, b. in Rochester, 1832, d. at St. Fe. [2] George B., b. 1834; [3] Oliver W., b. 1837; [4] Nora and Kathleen, died in infancy; [5] Charles A., 1844. Alexander died in St. Fe. The mother is living at St. Louis with her children.

IV. [3] *Jane P.*, b. in Hudson, Nov. 21, 1808; living in Hudson.

IV. [4] *George*, b. in Hudson, Sept. 15, 1810; living in California.

IV. [5] *James*, b. in Hudson, Dec. 25, 1812; d. in infancy.

IV. [6] *Susan*, b. in Hudson, June 1, 1814; married her kinsman, Justus McKinstry, son of David Charles (II.), and had five children, viz., Angelica and Susan H., both d. in infancy; [3] Charles F., b. 1843; [4] James H., b. 1845; [5] Carlisle, b. 1854.

Charles, b. in Hudson, Sept. 17, 1816; d. at Perry, Mo., April 14, 1841. He married Ellen H. Avery, and had one daughter, Cassandra, b. at Claverack, N. Y., 1840, and d. 1845. His widow married his brother, Augustus.

IV. [8] *John*, b. at Hudson, Sept. 9, 1818; d. Jan. 3, 1824.

IV. [9] *Augustus*, b. at Hudson, Dec. 5, 1821; is living at Hudson, 1865. He married his brother Charles's widow, and has four children, viz: Jeannie, b. Nov. 3, 1851, George A., b. Feb. 20, 1855, Nellie, b. Aug. 31, 1858, Sukie Victorine, b. April 10, 1862.

III. ELIZABETH, daughter of Col. John,[2] b. 1774; d. 1841; married Walter T. Livingston, of Livingston, N. Y., and had five children, viz:

IV. [1] *William R.*, b. May 1, 1799.

IV. [2] *Susan M.*, b. June 12, 1802; d. Aug. 20, 1805.

IV. [3] *Jane*, b. Sept. 4, 1804; married Hon. John Saunders, of Schenectady, and had three children, Walter T., Eugene L., and Mary E.

IV. [4] *Mary T.*, b. May 20, 1810; d. Dec 11, 1838.

IV. ⁵ *Susan*, b. May 4, 1816 ; married Peter Van Deusen, of Greenport, N. Y., and had Mary L., Anna, Jennie, Livingston, and one
died.

III. JOHN, son of Capt. John,² b. 1777 ; married, 1st, Elizabeth
Smith, in 1802, who d. June 21, 1819. 2d, Salome Root, March 16, 1820.
He died Sept. 30. 1846, leaving a widow and seven children, viz :
IV. ¹ *Mary Ann*, b. Oct. 11, 1802, resides in Greenport, N. Y.
IV. ² *William H.*, b. Oct. 20, 1804 ; married, 1st, Elizabeth Gavett, by
whom he had one child who died in infancy. By his 2d wife,
Elizabeth Like, he had four children, Edwin, Charles, Mary and
John. Mary, b. Dec. 1, 1854, d. Dec. 31, 1860. They live in
Hudson.
IV. ³ *Eliza*, b. June 25, 1807, mar. George Decker, of Stuyvesant, N.
Y., and had Jacob, who mar. Lucie Phillips, and lives in Green-
port. Helen, mar. to Peter Miller and lives in Hudson. Robert,
dead.
IV. ⁴ *Rachel*, b. Sept. 22, 1809 ; mar. Dr. Charles Skiff, of New
Haven, Conn., and had a son named Charles, and two daughters
by the name of Elizabeth who died young. Charles is mar. and
resides in Danbury, Conn., in the practice of medicine. His wife
was Susie R. Tweeds.
IV. ⁵ *Robert*, b. March 17, 1812 ; mar. Isabel Adelaide Bowles, Jan.
25, 1859, and had Victorine Estelle, Aug. 13, 1860 ; Everett,
Jan. 25, 1865. He lives in New York.
IV. ⁶ *John*, b. May 20, 1821, resides in Nelson, Ill.
IV ⁷ *Sloan*, b. July 28, 1828. Resides in Nelson, Ill.
Delia, a daughter of Capt. John, b. July 31, 1817, d. June 5, 1819.

III. WILLIAM, son of Col. John,² b. Dec. 25, 1779, d. Dec. 2, 1829 ;
married Rebecca Barnard, and had *Daniel P.* and *William C.*, who died
at sea. William C. married Amelia Luddington, and had four children.
Eliza, 3d child of William, married Walter B. Crane, and has two children, living with her at Rondout, N. Y.

III. HENRY, son of Col. John ² b. Oct. 10, 1782 ; married Julia
Day, widow of Capt. Gardiner, Sept. 17, 1807, by whom he had six child-
ren, viz :
IV. ¹ *Henry Day* b. June 29, 1808 ; d. 1809.
IV. ² *Philo*, b. March 14, 1810 ; d. 1810.
IV. ³ *Helen*, b. April 17, 1811 ; d. at Greenport, June 19, 1847. Sept.
1, 1829, she married William Griegs, of Greenport and had Julia
Sophia, b. June 28, 1831 ; d. Aug. 23, 1831 : and Edward, b.
Aug. 13, 1836 ; d. Jan. 22, 1864.

IV. [4] *Delia*, b. Sept. 1, 1813 ; d. Feb. 15, 1816.

IV. [5] *Edward II.*, b. Aug. 24, 1815 ; d. Aug. 11. 1836, at Catskill.

IV. [6] *Sherwood*, b. Aug. 4, 1823 ; d. Sept. 28, 1823, at Catskill. He is living at Greenport, in 1865 ; his wife died in 1864.

ANSEL, son of Col. John,[2] b. 1787 ; died at Hudson, 1865. He married, 1st, Sarah McKinstry, and had, [1] *Elizabeth*, b. 1817 ; d. young : a [2] *Son*, d. an infant ; and [3] *Delia*, b. 1821, d. 1833. By his 2d wife, Caroline Bemis, he has no issue.

III. ROBERT, son of Col. John,[2] b. 1774 ; married Sally Hammond and has no issue ; is now living at Hudson. His wife died 1862.

I find a third and distinct branch of the McKinstry family, which came to this country at a different time from either of the other two. They, as well as the others, went from the vicinity of Edinburgh to Ireland. The grand-father and father of *William*, the first of this branch who came to this country, emigrated from Scotland to Carrickfergus, in Ireland, prior to 1700. Of the common origin of the three branches of immigrants of this name, I can have no doubt although I have no direct proof of it. A great grand-son of William above named, writes me as follows :—" Our branch originated in Edinburg, and my Great-grand-father, (Wm.) knew that his kinsfolks had settled in this State, (Mass.) previous to his leaving Ireland. And one of the Ellington family visited at the house of David,[3] son of James II., and they traced back the relationship without difficulty. These parties are dead and their memorials have perished ; but Mrs. Lyon, a daughter of David McKinstry,[3] preserves the fact, and has no doubt of the relationship. Our next advance must be to find the main stock in Scotland and in the neighborhood of Edinburgh.

I. WILLIAM, born in Carrickfergus in 1722 ; immigrated to this country in 1740 or '41, and landed in Boston. He went to Medfield, where he remained about seven years. He then established himself in that part of Sturbridge which is now Southbridge, Mass., in 1748, on a farm, which has ever since been occupied by his descendants, in a direct line to the present day. In 1751 he married Mary Morse, by whom he had thirteen children, viz :

II. [1] *James*, married and had fifteen children, as hereinafter stated.

[2] *Sarah*, married Abel Bacon, and died in New York in 1814.

[3] *William*, married Esther Robbins, and has a family, as hereinafter stated.

[4] *Molly*, married Ephraim Bacon, and died without issue, 1828.

[5] *Amos*, was a soldier in the army of the revolution. He moved to Vermont, where he died in 1844, leaving a family. His sons are all dead.

[5] *John*, also a soldier in the army; married and moved to the neighborhood of Seneca Falls, in New York, where he died, leaving a family. Two of his sons only living. One, Horace H., in Stillwater, Minnesota, the other in Michigan.

[7] *Experience*, married Wm. Hobbs, and moved to Vermont, where she died, leaving issue.

[8] *Elizabeth*, married William Saunders, and died in Charlton, 1852.

[9] *Joseph*, died in Sturbridge, 1809, unmarried.

[10] *Margaret*, died in Southbridge, 1822. She married John Gray.

[11] *Alexander*, died in infancy.

[12] *Jane*, died in Sturbridge, 1793, unmarried.

[13] *Nathan*, a distinguished physician and surgeon, died in Newbury, Vt., unmarried, in 1815.

The following inscription is on his tomb-stone:

"Dr. Nathan McKinstry, Ob. Feb. 6, 1815, aged 41.
"Inurned beneath, there lies no quack,
But the dear ashes of good Doctor McK.,
Whose talents, taste and virtues could not save
His generous bosom from an earthly grave."

II. JAMES, the eldest son of William (I.), married Lois Dix in 1773, and died in Southbridge, Dec., 1819; his wife died Oct., 1815. By her he had thirteen children, viz:

III. [1] *James*, b. Jan., 1774, d. Jan., 1831; mar., 1st, Alice Fassett, of Conn., and had by her five children, two of whom died in infancy. His daughter Louisa, born in 1807, mar. John A. Parker, of Worcester, and died Sept., 1846, leaving three children, of whom one daughter, Frances Maria, living unmarried in California, only survives. He mar., 2d, Susan Shedd, of Vermont, and had seven children, 3 sons and 4 daughters.

III. [2] *Alexander*, b. April, 1775, mar. Sally Rider, of Charlton, Mass., and had a son, Wm. Pitt,[4] who mar. Ann Doubleday, and had two children, Calista, b. 1843, and William, b. 1845. Calista mar. Alanson Follansbee and d. without issue. His daughter, Mary Dale, mar. Rev. Alden Handy, and had a son William, who was lost at sea, and two daughters.

III. [3] *Anna*, b. Nov., 1776, d. Nov., 1830; mar. Ansel Dunbar, of Ludlow, Vt., and had eight children, four of whom died young. Her oldest son, Frederick,[4] b. 1804, mar. Lydia Warren, of Ludlow, and had ten children, six of whom are dead. By his 2d wife, Cornelia H. Childs, of Randolph, Vt., Frederick has no children. Her daughter Anna,[4] b. Oct., 1806, mar. John Warren, and settled in N. Y. She had ten children, four of whom died young. One of her sons, Ansel, mar. Helen Higbee.

Samuel,[4] son of Anna,[3] mar. Phebe Adams, of Vermont, and has 8 children. Austin,[4] another son of Anna,[3] mar. Nancy Tilden, of Ludlow, and has 6 children.

III. [4] *Lois*, b. May, 1778, d. Sept., 1846 ; mar. Norman Bates and had 6 children : he d. 1814, and she mar., 2d, Levi Mason, who d. in 1844, and she mar., 3d, Zebulon Spaulding, who d. in 1855, aged 85. Her son, Norman,[4] mar. Sally Pollard and had three children, who all mar. and had children, living in Vermont. Her son, Warner,[4] mar. Phebe Pettigrew, of Sherborn, Vt., and had six children. Her daughter, Elmira,[4] mar. Benj. F. Cummings, and had one daughter ; 2d, Rufus N. Barton, and had three children. Her daughter, Cornelia,[4] b. 1810, mar. Amos Boynton, of Vt., and had a son and two daughters.

III. [5] *Mary*. b. Oct., 1780, d. Dec., 1823 ; mar. Amos Putney, of Charlton, and had two sons and two daughters. Her son, Gerry,[4] b. 1804, mar. Elsy Gordon, a native of Maine, and had five children ; he died in Kanzas : her son, Jairus, b. 1809, mar. Mary P. Foster, of Charlton, and had 2 daughters, one d. in childhood, the other, Mary Foster, b. 1835, mar. George Hutchins, of Providence, R. I., and had four children.

III. [6] *William*, 6th child of James (II.), b. April, 1789, d. Nov., 1836, moved to West Newbury, Mass., where he mar. Lydia Tenney, and had two daughters, viz., *Elizabeth Smith*,[4] b. 1811, mar. Silas Follansbee and had one son who died in infancy, and *Lydia*,[4] b. 1815, mar. Wm. Cooper, and has no children.

III. [7] *Benjamin*, b. Oct., 1783, d. Sept., 1857 ; mar., 1st, Mary Howard, of Sturbridge, Mass., and had one son, Benj. F. ; they moved to West Newbury in 1810 ; the son died in 1837. He mar., 2d, Miriam M. George, daughter of John and Rachel George, of W. Newbury, by whom he had three children, *George W.* b. 1832, d. 1834 ; *Levi Carter*, b. Dec. 17, 1834, a Methodist minister in 1859, at Concord, N. H., and *Rebecca P.*, b. Sept. 23, 1837 ; mar. Leander Dodman, and lives in New Hampshire.

III. [8] *Nancy*, b. May, 1785, d. Dec., 1830 ; mar. Walter Woodward, of New Bedford, Mass., and had four children. Her oldest son, Addison,[4] b. 1809, mar. Mary Gould, of New Bedford, and had nine children ; her daughter Harriet P.,[4] b. 1821, mar. Moses Kimball, of New Bedford, and had three daughters ; two died young, the eldest Harriet,[5] mar. Wm. Richards. She mar. a 2d husband, Alfred M. Chapman. Her daughter, Nancy Maria,[4] mar. and died in 1848, without issue.

III. [9] *David*, b. March, 1780, d. in 1857 ; mar. Mary Clemance and lived and d. in Charlton ; he had a son and daughter. His son, Moses C.,[4] b. June, 1818, mar. Widow Polly B. Conant, and had one son, Sylvanus,[5] b in 1847, and one daughter, Susan,[5] b. 1816, mar. John Jones Bigelow, of Charlton, and had 2 children, b. in 1836 and 1840, the oldest, John, d. at his birth, the survivor is Andrew Le Roy. Mrs. Bigelow mar. a 2d husband, Calvin Lyon, of Charlton.

III. [10] *Daniel*, b May, 1788, d. April, 1841 ; mar. Rachel Brown, and had one son and 4 daughters ; his oldest daughter, Rachel,[4] b. Jan., 1815, d. in Charlton in March, 1858. Orrel D.,[4] b Jan., 1817, d. in Sturbridge, June, 1854, both leaving families. Rachel mar. James Flint, of Charlton, and had eight children. Orrel mar. 1st, Hiram Vinton, of Dudley, and had three children ; 2d, Samuel Shumway, of Sturbridge, and had a daughter, Ellen Augusta, b. July, 1853 ; Amity B.,[4] b. 1819, mar. Chandler Healy, of Dudley, and had two sons and two daughters ; one of her daughters, Mary Ann, b. 1838, mar. Durling M. Brownell, who was killed in the battle of the Wilderness, May 8, 1864, leaving two young children ; Diantha J.,[4] another daughter of Daniel,[3] b. 1821, mar. George Morse, of Southbridge, and had seven children, from 1841 to 1861, four sons and three daughters. Daniel, Jr.,[4] b. 1825, youngest son of Daniel,[3] mar. 1st, Abigail Stevens, of Charlton, and had two children, a son and daughter ; the daughter Novella, b. 1847, mar. —— Lilly, of Barre, 2d, Laura Greene, of Brimfield, and had two daughters.

III. [11] *Martha*, b. and d. 1790.

III. [12] *Moses*, b. 1792, d. same year.

III. [13] *Moses*, b. March, 1795, d. Aug., 1848 ; mar. Louisa Robinson, of Naushaun island, and had four sons and four daughters. His son, Moses W.,[4] b. 1821, mar. Widow Chapman ; has no children. Louisa,[4] b. 1823, mar. Palmer T. Bowen, and died in Sutton, without issue. Emily Ann,[4] b. 1825, mar. Samuel Prince, and d. in Providence, R. I , 1854, without issue. Eliza G.,[4] twin of Louisa, mar. Olney Howland, of Providence, and has two sons, Samuel, b. 1829, mar. Ellen J. Jones, and has two children. Leander S.,[4] b. 1833, mar. and has a son and two daughters. Ellen Phebe,[4] b 1837, mar. Nelson J. Smart and had three children, only one survives.

III. [14] *Andrew J.*, b. Feb., 1817, mar. Mary A. Dickey and had eight sons and two daughters ; his eldest son, Geo. Andrew,[4] b. Oct., 1836, and his youngest, John Fremont, Jan., 1857,—his eldest daughter, Mary, b. 1840, mar. Nathan W. Wellington and has one daughter b. 1865.

III. [15] *John A.*, died in infancy.

Descendants of this prolific family, James (II.), are very numerous and scattered far and wide over the country. To trace all the collateral branches would occupy more space than I have room for.

II. WILLIAM, 3d son of William (I.), married Esther Robbins, of Sturbridge, in 1785, and had children as follows, viz:

III. ¹ *John*, b. April, 1786, d. 1863.
    ² *Elizabeth*,, b. Sept., 1787, d. 1860.
    ³ *Mercy*, b. Feb., 1789.
    ⁴ *William*, b. July, 1792.
    ⁵ *Silas*, b. Aug., 1797, d. in 1856.

III. ¹ *John*, eldest son of William (II..), b. April, 1786, d. Dec., 1863. He mar. Keziah Batchelder, of Charlton, b. 1787, d. 1863, and had IV. *Prevostus*, b. Sept., 1809 ; *Manilla*, b. May, 1811 ; *William F.*, b. May, 1814 ; *John O.*, b. Sept , 1816 ; *Eliza*, b. June, 1821 ; *Mary*, b. 1823, d. Sept , 1827 ; *Caroline*, b. Aug., 1825. Prevostus, mar., 1st, Rosetta Hill, of Charlton, and had three sons, viz.. John Hill,⁵ 1835, mar. Mary McCracken, and lives in Iowa ; Elliot F.,⁵ served three years in the army, wounded and a prisoner at Balls Bluff, lives in Southbridge ; Martin Van,⁵ b. 1839, mar. Nancy Conant, 1859, and had two children, Julius, d. young, and Mellissa, b. 1862, survives. He was taken prisoner in Tennessee and has not been heard from since Dec., 1863. By 2d wife, Jane Carpenter, Prevostus had six children, four daughters and two sons.

IV. ² *Manilla*, mar. Vering Fisk, of Southbridge, and had nine children, six sons and three daughters, between 1832 and 1855, of whom four only survive, viz, John Davis,⁵ mar. Mary Morse, and has two children ; John F.,⁵ a member of Nim's battery during the war, and Edmund V ⁵ : Jane Kezia,⁵ b. 1739, mar. F. P. Pratt, Dec., 1860, and had two children, one, Francis, b. in 1862, the other, George, b. and d. in 1865 ; Frederick William,⁵ b. Sept., 1848, and Charles Albert,⁵ b, June, 1855 ; his son, George Francis,⁵ died in camp on Gallop's island in 1864.

    John's son, William F.,⁴ b. May, 1814, mar. Hannah H. Bacon, of Charlton, and had three daughters, Mary,⁵ Elizabeth and Alice.

IV. *John O.*, fourth child of John,³ b. Sept., 1816, mar. Eliza R. Spaulding, and had five children, viz., Charles Otis,⁵ b. 1847, d. Sept., 1849. John Willard,⁵ b. Nov., 1848. Eliza Jane,⁵ b. Oct., 1850. George Francis,⁵ b. Aug., 1852, d. 1855. Ira Jacobs,⁵ b. Dec., 1854. John O. is a merchant in Southbridge, and has represented his town in the Legislature. He lives on the homestead which has been in the family 115 years.

IV. *Eliza*, daughter of John,³ b. June, 1821, mar. Adam Miller who

d. in 1848, leaving two children, viz., William Frank,[5] who lives in Chicago, served three years in the 15th Mass. Reg., and Anna Eloisa,[5] b. 1843, mar. Orange S. Lee and lives in Southbridge, without issue. Eliza,[4] mar. 2d, Levi Bartlett, of Southbridge, in 1864.

IV. *Caroline*, youngest daughter of John,[3] b. 1825, mar. Adolphus Meriam and lives in Framingham, Mass ; had six children between 1849 and 1865, of whom, two daughters and three sons survive, unmarried.

III. *Elizabeth*, second child of William,[2] b. 1787, d 1860; mar. Asa Dresser, of Charlton, and had six children between 1810 and 1820, viz., Silas,[4] Calista, Julius, Julia, Miriam and Sylvester. Calista, Julius and Julia, died unmarried. *Silas*,[4] mar. Polly N. Hooker, Jan., 1835, and had eight children, four sons and four daughters ; his daughter Julia Elizabeth,[5] mar. Henry Harrington, Jr., and had two daughters, Jennie E. and Evart ; his daughter Martha,[5] mar. Dexter Harrington, 1857, and had two children, of whom Charles D.,[6] b. Oct., 1862, only survives , Silas's son Samuel,[5] mar. Nellie Palmer, May, 1864, and has one daughter, Nellie,[6] b. 1865 ; his daughter Miriam, mar. Ruggles W. Morse and has a son, Frederick D.,[6] b. Aug., 1865. Elizabeth's[3] daughter, Miriam,[4] mar. William S. Knowlton, Sept., 1837, and had one son, Julius W.,[5] b. Nov., 1838, and lives in Bridgeport, Conn. IV. Sylvester, the youngest and only surviving child of Elizabeth,[3] m. Nancy M. Morse, April, 1847, and had three daughters and one son from 1853 to 1863 ; the eldest daughter, Nellie, d. in 1854, the others are unmarried.

III. *Mercy*, 3d child of William,[2] mar. Luther Clemance, who d. in Southbridge. They had six children between May, 1817 and October, 1824, viz , *Harry*,[4] b. 1817, mar. Maryette Marsh, of Naples, N. Y., and had a son and daughter ; the daughter d. unmarried, in 1859, the son, George L.,[5] b. 1852. *John McK.*, b. 1820, mar. Elizabeth Broadstreet and had two sons and a daughter ; the eldest son, Charles L., b. 1853, d. 1854; Luther D., b. 1827, mar. Sarah Holmes, of Southbridge, and had a son, Charles Luther, b. 1864. Mercyette, 4th child of Mercy,[3] mar. Washington White, of Charlton, and had four daughters from 1856 to 1864. Lucian,[5] 6th child of Mercy,[3] mar. Mary F. Tufts, of Southbridge.

III. *William*, 4th child of William,[2] b. July, 1792, mar. Matilda Marcy, and had six children, born between 1815 and 1829, inclusive. *Esther*,[4] the eldest, mar. Aretas Hooker and d. in 1860, leaving two children, viz., William H.,[5] mar. Susan Taft, Dec., 1863, and has a daughter, Hetta Matilda, b. 1865, and

Esther Matilda,[5] mar. John Spenser, and lives in Enfield, Conn.,
with two children, William.[6] and Matilda, b. 1863 and 1864.

IV. *Elijah*, b. July, 1816, d. April, 1860, unmarried.

IV. *Nathan*, 3d child of William,[3] mar. Hannah Taylor, and had six
children between 1844 and 1858, of whom four sons and one
daughter survive, unmarried.

IV. *John A.*, 5th child of William,[3] b. 1825, mar. Widow Sarah H.
Pratt, of Vt., and has one son, Charles Sumner, b. 1860.

IV. *William*, 4th child of William,[3] b. 1821, mar. Mary Ann Kitchen,
and has one son and three daughters, b. 1847 to 1861, unmarried.

IV. *Mary*, youngest child of William,[3] b. 1829, mar. George Brackett,
and died in Sturbridge, without issue.

III. *Silas*, 3d child of William,(II.) married Lucy Twiss, of Charlton, and had seven children, of whom three sons and one daughter died unmarried. *Albert*,[4] his eldest son, b. June, 1820, mar.
Sarah J. Edwards in 1860 : no children. *Henry*,[4] b. Nov., 1822
James T.,[4] b. May, 1827.

II. *Amos*, 5th child of William,(I.) mar. Miss Pike, and moved to
Vermont, where he died in 1844. His two sons, Amos and
George are both dead. He has several daughters who married
and have families in high social standing, near Hyde Park, Vt.
Amos,[2] was a soldier in the revolution.

II. *John*, 6th child of William.(I.) was also a soldier in the revolu-
tion ; he mar. Catherine Slaughter and lived near Seneca Falls,
N. Y. He had eleven children, eight sons and three daughters,
who are all dead but Horace K.,[3] living in Nebraska, and
Benaiah,[3] in Michigan, both married ; Benaiah to Elizabeth
Boice, Horace to Delocia E. Carpenter, of Woodstock, Conn.
Four sons died unmarried ; the three daughters were married.

III. *Horace K.*, son of John,(II.) had five children, viz., John L.,
mar. Adelia Northrop, of St. Anthony's Falls, Min. ; Eliza Jane,
mar. Seth M. Sawyer, of Stillwater, Min. ; Adelaide, mar.
Thomas E. Cassidy ; Catherine O., mar. Henry Seeley ; Mary
Virginia, unmarried.

II. *Elizabeth*, 8th child of William,(I.) mar. William Saunders and
d. in Charlton in 1852. She had five children, viz., [1]William,
[2]McKinstry, [3]James, [4]Moses, [5]Mary. Mary mar. Mr. Dick-
inson, of North Hampton, Mass., and has one son, Frederick,
living in Charlton, unmarried.

II. *Margaret*, 10th child of William,(I.), d. in Southbridge in 1822.
She mar. John Gray, of Charlton, and had six children, viz ,
Henry, Amarillis, Aurelia, John, Saphira and Harrison Otis.

The numerous members of this branch, from what I believe to be a common stock, springing from the midlands of Scotland, and now contributing by their industry, intelligence and skill, to build up the towns and waste places of our western world, had their primal seat in this country, at Southbridge, where many of the elder race remain to preserve and perpetuate the sound principles they inherited from their virtuous ancestors. I hope this imperfect notice will incite them or some of them to collect and transmit full details of all branches of this respected and honorable family.

The name still lives in the neighborhood of Edinburg as well as in various parts of Ireland.

Col. McKinstry, of the English Army, is now in service in the British possessions in America, and I find that *Henry McKinstry* was elected Mayor of Hamilton, in Canada West, in 1860. I have not been able to ascertain what stock these gentlemen are from.

NOTE.—In revising my work for this new edition, at the close of the unparalleled war through which we have passed, I have been impressed by the fact, that, as the war of the revolution, which gave us a National existence, members of the different branches of our race, bore important parts, so in the recent struggle for the preservation of that existence, their descendants have as freely and honorably perilled their lives. In these noble efforts, several have perished either in combat or by other contingencies of war. Some of these I have briefly noticed, as their names have occurred in the order of my narrative; of others, of whom I would have gladly spoken, I have no particular information. One, however, has come to my knowledge while the last pages were going to press, concerning whom I will not omit the opportunity of a brief notice. Surgeon *Robert A. Babbitt* was the eldest son of Emily, daughter of Alvin McKinstry, the son of Paul, who was the youngest son of the Rev. John of Ellington. There was united in him, with the blood of the McKinstrys, that of the Rev. Thomas Smith, the first pastor of the first church in Portland, through his daughter Lucy, wife of Thomas Sanders, of Cape Ann. He graduated at the Medical College at Albany, in 1860. In 1861 he joined the 8th Conn. Regiment of Volunteers as a private, and was appointed its hospital steward. In 1862, he was appointed Superintendent of the Hammond General Hospital at Beaufort, N. C. In 1863, he was promoted Surgeon of the 1st N. C. Union Volunteers having its head quarters at Washington, N. C. In 1864, he received the appointment of Post Surgeon at Beaufort, where, in consequence of extensive and fatal disease, his labors were excessive, in which his health gave way, and he perished of yellow fever, Oct. 17, 1864, in the 23d year of his age. The Vermont State Journal, in an appreciative notice of this excellent young man, says, "Though young in years, he proved himself eminently successful and efficient in his profession, and a faithful and devoted soldier to his country." Similar testimonials could be offered in behalf of various other members of our family, who nobly gave themselves to the cause of their country in the hour of her peril. Among these were Capt. James P. McKinstry. of the Navy, whose gallant passage of Port Hudson is on the page of history, the youthful Arthur McKinstry, grand-son of Perseus, who, after many battles, perished in the great struggle at Williamsburg. Henry W. Wells, a descendant of Dr. Wm. McKinstry, having served gallantly in the Navy, was lost at sea in command of a National vessel. Capt. Samuel W. Duncan, a volunteer in the Army of the Mississippi; he united two streams of the Scotch Irish blood Duncan and McKinstry. And Commander Francis Winslow, of the Navy, a noble and brave officer who mingled the stock of the revolutionary hero, *Stark* with that of the McKinstry.

I find that each branch of the McKinstrys has contributed of its Sons to the patriotic cause of the Country, as appears in the preceding genealogy and will be borne upon the great roll of honor. Of these, are Alexander McKinstry, the great grand-son of Paul; Durling M. Brownell, killed in the battle of the Wilderness; John F. Fisk, a member of the famed Nim's battery, and Frederick Wm. Fisk; Elliott F. McKinstry served honorably three years; Martin Van McKinstry, a prisoner and probably a victim, as he has not been heard from George Francis Fisk died in Camp, and Wm. Frank Adams. All young and enthusiastic, they offered themselves to the great cause. The last seven were descendants from William,(I.) the immigrant from Carrickfergus.

The same spirit which inspired the hearts of the Sires in the *first* revolution, was not abated in their sons in the *second*. The union of the Scotch, the Celt and the Saxon in this race form enduring elements of harmony and strength.

INDEX.